Ya Got People

Helping people with developmental disabilities deal with grief,
bereavement and loss

Written By
Carolyn S. Bowling
and
Jeffrey W. Wilder

Diverse City Press

www.diverse-city.com

© Copyright 2003
by
Diverse City Press
All Rights Reserved

Printed in Canada

Cover Design by Michael Soucie

Cover Art by "Diane"

Bowling, Carolyn S. and Wilder, Jeffery W.
Ya Got People: Helping people with developmental
disabilities deal with grief, bereavement and loss.

1: Grief
2: Developmental Disability
3. Counseling / Therapy

ISBN 1-896230-26-1

This book is dedicated to
Johnny Bowling and Wayne Bennett,
whose deaths greatly impacted our
understanding of
and our response to
grief, bereavement and loss

TABLE OF CONTENTS

Carolyn: People come to various crossroads at different points in their lives. Their experiences, be they personal, professional, or both, lead them down a certain path. Thus is the case with Jeff and me. Each of us became aware of loss at a very early age. My own first awareness of loss came probably around the age of 3 or 4. My grandmother lived in "very rural" Amherst County, Virginia. She lived in walking distance of the Baptist church and felt it her "civic" duty to attend every funeral at the church. She took me along. I wasn't scared. I was curious about the "why" of all those flowers and all those crying people. Grandmother explained that people send flowers out of love for the family, and that people cry out of love for the one who is dead. I heard it in my head, but not in my heart until the death of my beloved grandfather when I was age 10. It was then that I understood loss all too well. My grandfather's death was the beginning of a long death history, which would be most impacted by the suicide of my younger brother, Johnny, at age 30. The grief that I experienced as a result of his life and death is the impetus behind my current work in the field of grief and bereavement.

Jeff: My first awareness of loss was most likely the death of a pet. Our pet parakeet made a break for freedom, leaving the warmth of our kitchen and flying into a cold November night. I cried myself to sleep over that one. On the human front, the death of my cousin, Wayne, made a lasting impression on me. He was electrocuted while working on a piece of farm equipment. Until Wayne died, death had always seemed to be a distant thing. I knew that old people died but, with Wayne's death, I realized that young people could die. I could die. So began my acquaintance with grief, bereavement and loss.

In the late 1980's there were a great number of deaths at our hospital, and surrounding community, in a relatively short period of time. Carolyn and I joined forces and conducted several grief and bereavement workshops for caregivers. Our outlooks on life, and our personal styles were very similar, and we had a great working chemistry. We also had a great deal of fun working together. Because of job changes and individual responsibilities, our paths separated. Of course, we worked together on the hospital, when the need arose, and when someone died, but not on a consistent basis. That changed in 1997, when Carolyn asked if I would be interested in co-leading grief and bereavement seminars. She had been a very busy lady, professionally. Over the past several years, she had been attending a series of grief and bereavement workshops, and had gathered quite an impressive store of resources. Carolyn put together a wonderful seminar and presented it at our place of employment. People from across the state of Virginia, who work with people with disabilities, attended and were impressed with her presentation. She had been discovered!

Carolyn started receiving requests to travel to other areas and share her material with employees wanting to learn how to better cope with death, grief and bereavement. There was just one hitch. Being legally blind, Carolyn needed a driver. She asked if my boss (another wonderful Carolyn) might allow me to travel with her and be her "wheels." Oh, yes, she also thought it would be fun to co-teach. The opportunity was just too good to resist. My boss (that other Carolyn) thought it was a great idea, and agreed to let me do it.

Several presentations later, Carolyn and I were invited to conduct a day-long grief and bereavement seminar at HPR III, in October of 1998, in Roanoke, Virginia. The seminar was well received. The participants did have a request, however. They asked that we include more material, specifically concerning people with disabilities, and their grief in future presentations. Carolyn and I immediately began brainstorming about stories and materials that we could include. As we talked, we realized two things.

The first thing we realized was that we wanted to expand the concept of grief beyond death and dying. Grief is a universal process and people with disabilities are not exempt. Our challenge is to figure out "how" each person expresses that grief. Also important is the grief experienced by family members and caregivers. The second thing that we realized was that we already had a wealth of resources to draw from...ourselves. Carolyn is an albino, and visually impaired. I have cerebral palsy, and "Special K" legs (that's a cereal by Kellogg). We now had the beginnings of an expanded presentation. Enter, Dave Hingsburger.

Being employed by the state of Virginia, we could not be paid for our presentation, but we were told that we could stay an extra day and attend any presentation of our choice. We decided to attend a communication workshop, led by Dave Hingsburger. Dave is a wonderful story teller, and a sincere advocate for people with disabilities. Carolyn and I thoroughly enjoyed his workshop, and told him so, before we left to return to Lynchburg, Virginia.

The following Monday, I was surprised to find a note in my mailbox to call Dave. I had no clue whatever as to why he wanted to talk to me. Then, it hit me. I had been somewhat disruptive in his workshop, and I figured that he was calling to make sure that I never attended another one. Imagine my shock when we finally connected and Dave asked if Carolyn and I would consider writing a book of stories about how people with disabilities deal with grief, bereavement and loss issues. To my surprise, I heard a voice that sounded very much like mine saying, "Sure. We'll give it a try." When I hung up the phone, it occurred to me that I had not asked Carolyn what *she* thought about such a project. I called and left a message on her answering machine, telling her that I had told Dave that we would undertake to write a book for him. It was *her* turn to be speechless. Once she had recovered, however, she decided that she liked the idea.

So, here we are, three years later, having put forth our best effort. As we have attempted to tell these stories, one truth has become very clear. Grief for people with disabilities is no different than grief for anyone else. When you think about it, if we live long enough, we will all experience some degree of disability. What *may* be different is the creativity needed to help someone with a disability find a means of expression for his or her grief.

Carolyn and I have tried to tell these stories in a simple, conversational style. We have also made an effort to emphasize the main points of each story, and to provide some useful tools for your grief, bereavement and loss toolbox. We have also included some "power tools" in each chapter for your personal use. Many of them can be used in a variety of ways. Many of the power tools call for thought and introspection. They lend themselves to discussions with close friends and small groups. Keeping a journal of your thoughts is also an option. Others may be done as individual or group activities, and as a basis for discussion. Feel free to be as creative as your imagination allows. We believe that close examination of your own feelings and experiences regarding grief, bereavement and loss is necessary in order to better assist others.

Carolyn and I have not attempted to write the definitive book on grief, bereavement and loss among people with disabilities. We have simply tried to share some of our stories and experiences in as honest and straight forward a manner as possible. It is our hope that they might provide some insight and encouragement to those who care for people with disabilities and are attempting to help them cope with grief, bereavement and loss. We also hope that this book might inspire others to share their stories and experiences in written form.

Names mentioned in our stories have either been changed for confidentiality reasons, or we have received permission to use actual names. Just for fun, we won't tell you whether they're actual names, or ones we thought up ourselves. We hope that you enjoy traveling down a part of the road that we, and those we write about, have walked.

ACKNOWLEDGMENTS

Carolyn and I would like to thank Dave Hingsburger for this opportunity to stretch and grow. We would also like to thank our families for their love and support, which engendered within us the belief that we could accomplish whatever we put our minds to. Thanks also go out to our friends and co-workers, who listened to us, read our rough drafts, made suggestions, and offered encouragement and prayers as we worked on this book. Of course, we are indebted to those who appear within these pages. We hope that their stories will help you along your journey. We hope that we have been faithful in telling their stories. We gain strength from the knowledge that we do not travel this highway alone. Jeff and I thank you for your willingness to expand your horizons by reading our book. We would like to encourage you to reflect upon your own losses as you share the stories which follow, and to acknowledge those people who have helped you along your road.

In Jeremiah 31:21 the ancient prophet encouraged his people

to "set up waymarks for yourself, make yourselves guideposts; consider well the highway, the road by which you went." The writing of this book has provided the opportunity for the two of us to do just that. We draw strength from the knowledge that we do not travel this highway of life alone. Every person on the face of this earth, regardless of nationality, gender, race, creed, faith or disability, walks this road along with us. We leave you with these words from an unknown author:

"Life is a sacred journey and it is about change, growth, discovery, movement, transformation, continuously expanding our vision of what is possible, stretching our souls, learning to see clearly and deeply, listening to our intuition, taking courageous risks and embracing challenges along the way. We are on the path. Exactly where we are meant to be right now. And from here we can only go forward, shaping our life stories into a magnificent tale of triumph, of healing, of courage, beauty, wisdom, power, dignity and love."

Grief, bereavement and loss are universal emotions that, sooner or later, we all experience. People with disabilities are no exception. These emotions are a part of the human condition. The word "bereavement" has its roots in an Anglo-Saxon word meaning, "to be robbed." When we are faced with a significant loss, we often feel robbed, and we grieve for what we have lost. So, too, do persons with disabilities. Many individuals with disabilities are acutely aware of loss from an early age, which compounds with what life's situations provide.

Take, for example, the individual who, at a very early age has been "transplanted" from home (some have never been home and are transferred from a hospital shortly after birth) to an institution or other form of living arrangement. Losses such as not having any "say so" over where they live and who will take care of them; living a lifetime of segregation from others who label them as "different," or "not a part of"; the absence or loss of abilities. I (Carolyn) never really thought about leaving my home and family when I went to a residential school at age five. It was an exciting time for me and I adjusted well, until I went home for the first time, eight weeks later. I realized that I no longer lived there. Having to leave my home and family filled me with a great sadness. That sadness of "leaving" persisted throughout college and graduate school.

There are many ways in which grief is manifested (shock, sadness, anger, denial, bargaining, depression, painful longing, acceptance, etc.). Some of the losses we face include loss of family members, home, community, loss of control over our person/property, loss of sexuality, etc. People with disabilities grieve the loss of these things, too, often at a much earlier age. People with disabilities also grieve over lost abilities, labeling, and prejudice, among other things. Sometimes, their grief spans a lifetime.

To illustrate just how people with disabilities may experience grief at an earlier age than their non-disabled contemporaries, I (Jeff) would like to share an example from my own life. I grieve the loss of mobility. My cerebral palsy causes me to have extremely tight leg muscles. Walking is difficult. It took me three times longer to learn to walk than it does for the average person. Even then, I had to wear leg braces. As a child, I knew that, no matter what kind of sneaker I wore, I would never run faster or jump higher. Competing in sports was only a dream. I knew that I would always be picked last to play on a team, if at all. As an adult, I gave up a position as an interim youth minister because I simply could not physically keep up with my very active group of young people. (Not to mention that I was cramping my teenaged son's style.) Trying to participate in all of their activities caused me to experience significant pain. The emotional pain of having to admit to myself that I wasn't up to the physical challenge was equally painful. As hard as it was to gain mobility, it is proving incredibly easy to lose it. At 47 years of age I am thinking of buying a motorized chair because of the difficulty of walking long distances. Most people would not have to consider doing so until a much later age.

For people with disabilities, as with all people, the experience of grief is unique and varied for each individual. Our challenge is to figure out "how" each person expresses their grief. Differences in verbal and expressive ability, mental and emotional capacity, physical health, etc. can make this a difficult task, but we must try. We may simply need a bit more flexibility, creativity, and openness to do it well. If the grief, bereavement and loss· experiences of those with disabilities are not recognized and accepted, we may hinder or halt the expression of the feelings and emotions connected with them. This in turn may have an adverse effect on their social, emotional, and spiritual growth.

Eadie, for example, was unable to attend her mother's funeral. We talked with her family and decided to bring the funeral to her. The family had taken pictures at the funeral and brought them when they came to visit. Eadie's sisters showed her each picture and talked about the funeral service. Though Eadie was nonverbal, her expressions and gestures made it clear that she understood what was said and that she was glad that her family had come and shared the photographs with her.

We can help people with disabilities cope with grief, bereavement, and loss in the same way as we do anyone else. We can recognize that their grief exists, give them permission to express their grief, accept their expression, and give them physical, emotional, social and spiritual support. To demonstrate this, we offer the following story.

THE STORY

"Experts...*us?*" Jeff and I looked at each other in surprise after Carol's call. She had attended one of our Grief and Bereavement seminars, and she felt that we possessed the skills to help her out. Carol had called to ask if we would come to Reva, Virginia, and do some "Grief Work" at their Day Support Services Center.

Raymond, one of the participants in the day support program there, was dying of cancer. Staff were concerned as to how the 40 other participants in the day support program, who knew and loved Raymond, would react to his death. Carol also wanted us to visit Raymond's residence and talk with his three roommates and the staff who assisted them. One roommate eagerly helped Raymond any way he could. Another was angry. The third was silent and withdrawn. Carol wanted us to help them examine their feelings about Raymond's impending death, and to help them explore ways in which they could support Raymond and one another. This was the agenda when Jeff and I left Lynchburg and headed to Reva.

When we arrived at the Day Support Services Center, the receptionist, a young man, greeted us with a smile and asked what we wanted. When we had introduced ourselves, explained why we were there and who we were looking for, he got up from his seat, walked to the entrance to he hallway and shouted, "Ya got people here!" Joyce, the woman Carol had told us to ask for, came out and welcomed us to the Center. She led us into a conference room and told us that the mother of Lynn and Susan, two young ladies who came daily to the Center, had died of cancer the day before. Joyce wanted to know if Jeff and I would talk with Lynn and Susan. Their family, and the Center staff were not sure of how well the two sisters were coping with their mother's death. They were also not sure if Lynn and Susan would attend the "wake" and/or the funeral.

Lynn and Susan came into the conference room with Carol and sat down beside Jeff and me. Carol stayed with us so that they would feel more comfortable. Her affection for the young women was obvious. Lynn was very talkative, and speaking for herself and for her sister, too. Susan, on the other hand, was quiet, and said very little. Her eyes, however, were full of life and took in everything. Lynn told us up front that her "Mama" had died. The family had told them that their mother had the flu, and Lynn told us how scary it had been to sit by her bed and hold her hand. She was afraid that she might catch the flu and die like her mother had. Jeff and I were able to explain to Lynn and Susan that their mother had died of cancer, and that they could not "catch" it. That seemed to make them feel better. They also seemed to draw comfort from the knowledge that they were going to stay at Carol's home for awhile.

When asked if she and her sister wanted to attend the "wake" or the funeral, (Jeff and I explained to her what happens at each) she said, "No." without hesitation. It wasn't that she was afraid. It was simply that she and her sister had already seen their mother's body, and that was enough for them. We asked Lynn what kinds of things she liked to do and she told us that she liked to color. I asked her if she would color something for me. When she and Susan were ready to leave, Lynn gave me a beautiful mandala, which I have framed and on my desk to remind me of Lynn and of her courage.

Our "Agenda" had suddenly changed. After suggesting ways that they could continue to support Lynn and Susan, the staff asked Jeff and me if we would consider talking with the 40 other people who came to the day program. We readily agreed to do so. We had arrived at 10:00a.m. By the time the fourth group of 10 had left, it was almost 2:00p.m. With each group, personal grief experiences poured forth, like cleansing waters, refreshing anew.

"I know what death is." Mary said in a no nonsense tone. She told of going to her mother's funeral, along with the rest of the family. As she stood by her mother's casket, weeping, she heard the minister ask someone from her family, "What's *she* crying for?" The pain of that experience, and the emotional scars left behind were evident on Mary's face as she told her story. When she had finished, she informed the group, "I have to go outside for a few minutes and cry." What Jeff and I did not know was that her mother had died over 10 years ago. Mary had never discussed her mother's death, or shared her grief with anyone in all those years. In fact, since the day of her mother's funeral, she had not shed a single tear. The minister's question had made her feel that she was not *supposed* to cry. Mary told us later how glad she was that we had come. She said, "I feel so much better now!" After 10 years of silent grieving, she felt like she would be okay because she had "cried it out."

"I hate Christmas!" was the comment that came out of the blue from Hector. He'd been silent up until this point. Tears streamed from his eyes and it was, at times, difficult to understand his words through his sobs. His father had suffered a heart attack in the middle of Christmas dinner and died. Hector's pain stabbed at my own heart, because my father, too, had died at Christmas. I empathized with Hector's struggles to make it through the Christmas season. I asked him what helped him to cope, to which he replied, "I bake things and take them to people in the nursing homes." All through the year, Hector made sure that every staff person, and his fellow participants in the day program, had a card and gift for their birthday. During the Christmas season, everyone returned his kindness by taking special care of him.

Vivian sat beside me. She didn't say a word, but sobbed with each story told. I put my arm around her, rubbed her back and offered her tissues. She never did share, in words, what was on her mind, or in her life's experience, but we both felt the comfort and support that passed between the two of us.

"Ya know, some people just don't *get* it!" David was the definite leader in his group, and had his own agenda. Up to this point, we had talked about everything *but* death. We had talked about everything from Elvis to Sesame Street. Jeff and I were intrigued. "Tell us," we said, "What is it that people just don't get?" "Well," David replied, "When you're dead, you're gone, and that's it! So, you'd better be ready." David's friend, Ed, who had sat silently beside him the entire time, raised his hand and said, "Well, I, for one, *get* it!" From his tone of voice, Jeff and I had no doubt that he did, indeed, *get* it.

Marvin, one of David's friends, turned out to be an Elvis impersonator. Before Jeff and I left, he entertained us with his version of "Hound Dog," complete with microphone, sunglasses and his best Elvis impression. What Marvin didn't realize was that he had provided the "Comic Relief" that would give Jeff and me renewed strength for the next part of our journey.

We were off to Raymond's house, forewarned that Margaret, one of Raymond's housemates, was probably going to cuss us out when we mentioned the "d" word, as she had done with the Hospice workers. Oh, well, call us anything, as long as you call us for dinner!

Late arrivals and delayed dessert make wonderful opportunities for conversation around the table. Lunch had been saved for Jeff and me. After we had eaten lunch, we shared dessert with Raymond's housemates and caregivers. Raymond was not feeling well, and was in bed. The caregivers freely admitted that, until Raymond's illness, they had not thought about such things as their own death, what they wanted for burial arrangements, or about how those left behind to grieve would feel. Raymond's impending death was a rude awakening for some.

At first, Margaret did not join us at the table. She sat on the arm of a living room chair, just at the edge of the dining room, looking at Jeff and me with curiosity. I could tell that she was taking in everything that was being said. Every now and then, Jeff or I would ask her a question, inviting her to be a part of the conversation. We made sure that Margaret knew that she did not have to answer if she did not choose to. Before I knew it, she was seated beside me at the table. She did not cuss us out. In fact, she seemed to accept our presence in her home. Up to this point, Margaret had seemed angry at Raymond's coming death. The house staff told us that she had not been visiting Raymond in his room like his other housemates did when they returned home from work, or church. A few days after our visit, we were told that Margaret had finally gone into Raymond's room and sat with him in silence, seeming to be more at peace.

Jeff and I talked all the way back to Lynchburg. As it turns out, the most important lesson we learned was what the receptionist said when we first arrived at the Day Support Services Center in Reva: "Ya got people here!" As long as we remember that, the rest will take care of itself.

THE POINTS:

➡   **Table The Labels.** Fortunately for all of us, disability does not equal "*inability*". When Mary was crying at her mother's funeral and the minister asked, "What's she crying for?" he was labeling her display of emotion as "inappropriate" and her presence at the funeral as "unwanted." While it may be more difficult for some with disabilities to share thoughts and feelings, it is not impossible. People are not their disabilities. We must encourage people with disabilities to show us and to tell us who they are and how they grieve.

I have often heard phrases like, "He's a wheelchair". "She's Alzheimer's". "They're behaviors". I try to picture in my mind what on earth they're talking about. Can you imagine someone as a wheelchair? Now that would be one for the surrealists (oops, another label!)! One day a group of students with visual impairments were returning home from school. Someone looked out of the window and said, "The blinds are back." Silly me! I didn't even know we had sent them out to be cleaned!

The mindset of the past has been focused on labeling everything. I'm appalled when I read old records dating from the 1920's to the 1960's that were "politically correct" for their day. People with developmental disabilities were labeled as "morons," "imbeciles" and "idiots." These labels were developed by psychiatrists, psychologists, social workers and physicians, and were meant to define levels of intelligence. Instead, these labels became terms of derision and ridicule. This kind of labeling led us down a slippery slope to a place where society saw eugenics as a "service to society" and resulted in the sterilization of thousands of developmentally disabled individuals who had no voice because they "didn't matter"! Sadly, we continue to do the same thing today. Prejudice is taught. When groups of people are labeled, and we accept those labels, we begin to see jokes, comments and political policies directed toward those groups as "socially acceptable". They are not.

Whenever we label individuals or groups, we dehumanize them. Labels like "Japs", "Gooks", "Yanks", "The Great Satan", "Towel Heads", "Mentally Deficient", etc. help to make wars and discriminatory policies more "palatable". Labels lead to segregation. It's time for integration. Labels lead to exclusion. It's time for inclusion. Along with so many other groups of human beings, people with developmental disabilities are seeking to be integrated and included as full members of the world community. The time is now. We must all do our part to EDUCATE, ADVOCATE and INNOCULATE against the prejudices and practices of the past, present and future.

We've come a long way, baby, but we're not there yet! As an example of how far we've come, The Americans with Disabilities Act prohibits interviewers from asking "how" a job will be done when they are interviewing someone with a disability. I (Carolyn) would have appreciated having a level playing field all those years ago when I went for interviews and people were trying to figure out how I was going to "read" and "write".

Persons with disabilities have their own prejudices, too. Some do not wish to be with other persons with disabilities, do not wish to be identified as a person with a disability, and do not want any accommodations, even when such accommodations would be helpful to them.

Some of us band together in various Rights and Advocacy groups. We can be down right radical! The American Federation for the Blind has taught me a lot about standing up for my rights as a person with visual impairments. You've heard of the "Deaf Culture" who have their own rules and regulations. The Association for

Retarded Citizens is very proactive in working toward inclusion for persons with developmental disabilities. What strikes me as so funny is that I and other friends of mine who are blind or visually impaired can make what we call "blind" jokes, such as calling each other "blind blinkies", when we can't find something, but somebody with sight had better not go there! I have often said that if the whole world were blind, there would be no prejudice.

People with disabilities can be just as insensitive as our non-disabled contemporaries. I (Jeff) have a friend I dearly love and have a great deal of respect for. She has very strong hands, which I jokingly attributed to her years of work on the farm. I gave her several farm related labels, which I thought were playful and clever. After about a year of teasing her in this manner, I found out, from someone else, that my "playful" remarks hurt her deeply. Needless to say, the teasing stopped. This story is a perfect example of the need for self-advocacy. Had my friend told me that she was hurt and offended by my remarks, I would have stopped, immediately. Instead, she endured a year of emotional discomfort. All of us, disabled or not, need to speak up for ourselves when we are offended. Sometimes we do things, not in meanness, but in ignorance. People can't change their behavior if they don't know that they have offended. We must have open, honest dialogue with one another. For those who cannot speak for themselves, we must be their voices.

➡ **Everybody Grieves Somebody Sometime.** If we live long enough, grief will touch all of our lives. As Mary showed us, absence of tears does not mean absence of grief. Though it took her 10 years to allow herself to shed tears on the outside, there is no doubt that she had never stopped crying on the inside.

➜ **People Believe What They Perceive.** Jeff and I were called on as grief "experts." We are perceived as such simply because we have spent a great deal of time listening to and learning from those who are willing to share their stories. We also read, attend workshops, and share the things that others teach us. One thing that the staff in Reva told us was that they never knew that the people they served felt the way that they did. In fact, they were so excited by the stories and feelings that were shared that day that they asked if we would be willing to go to other Day Support Centers in the area and do the same kind of thing that we did there. We assured them that they could do what we did. The truth is that no one knows everything there is to know about a given subject. You, too, can become an "expert" if you are willing to listen, learn and share of yourselves with others.

➜ **Don't Reign On Someone's Pain.** No, that's not a typo. To reign over someone is to have control over them. It is tempting to want to protect people with disabilities. Often, their grief and pain make us uncomfortable. It is easy to say, "Don't cry. Don't grieve. Don't hurt." To be human is to cry, to grieve and to hurt. Always remember, "Ya got people here."

➜ **Recognition Leads To Permission.** When we went to Reva, we saw the people there as people who needed to grieve and share their stories. Having their grief recognized gave them permission to open up to us and to each other. We encouraged the people there to tell their stories their way...or not to tell them. We did our best to listen without judgment. We affirmed their grief, no matter how many years had passed since their loss had occurred. Time, alone, does not heal all wounds. People's need to grieve significant losses must be recognized, so that they will risk being vulnerable...especially people with disabilities.

➡ **Surrendah Your Agenda.** Jeff and I left Lynchburg with one agenda in mind, only to arrive in Reva to find that something different was needed. The willingness and ability to change our direction and approach to match the needs of those we seek to serve is a must.

➡ **Care Giving And Taking.** Carol, one of the staff from the Day Support Center, opened the door for Jeff and me to talk with Lynn and Susan. Because they loved and trusted Carol, they more easily came to trust us. One of the truly beautiful things that we saw repeatedly was the care that the day program participants gave to each other as they shared their grief. One lady, in particular, touched me. She got up from her place at the table and came around to the other side of the room. She sat beside a sobbing woman who was sharing her grief experience with us, reached out, and gently took her hand. She said, simply, "She's my best friend." By caring for one another in the midst of their grief, the people in Reva learned that they could give care, as well as receive it. They also found that they had the strength to cope with their losses. They moved from being "victims" to being "victorious." After Hector's father died at Christmas, Hector could have retreated into himself and isolated himself from others. Instead, he reached out to people by making sure everyone at his day support program had a birthday card and a gift. Instead of allowing his grief immobilize him every Christmas, Hector baked cookies for people in nursing homes. He also graciously accepted the kindnesses shown to him by his friends at Christmastime. He is a perfect example of the "give and take" of caregiving.

➜ **Just The Facts, Sir. Just The Facts.** Susan and Lynn's family thought that cancer, which you *can't* catch, was too scary, so they told them their mother had the flu, which you *can* catch. Now, *that's* scary! There is no substitute for the truth.

TOOLS YOU NEED FOR YOUR TOOLBOX

1. Openness and flexibility
2. Willingness to listen
3. A sense of humor
4. Appropriate touch
5. Acceptance of those who choose not to express their grief
6. Foster an atmosphere which encourages peers to comfort one another
7. Respect for an individual's right to choose whether or not to participate in grief rituals (wakes, funerals, etc.)
8. Respect for individual grief styles
9. Willingness to throw away the "rule book"
10. Recognition of persons with disabilities as people who grieve
11. Willingness to examine your own grief experiences
12. Knowledge of your feelings about grief, bereavement and loss
13. Awareness of things that push your "grief buttons"
14. Honesty

POWER TOOLS

Ⓟ   Perform a role play based on Mary's experience at her mother's funeral. Discuss feelings and issues raised.

Ⓟ   Recall a time when you needed to express significant sadness or grief, but were unable to do so. What feelings did you have? What did you need? What would you like to have said or done? What would you have liked from others?

Ⓟ   What is your most difficult loss to date? Who helped you? What changes occurred in your life as a result of this loss? How do you cope with loss? What benefits, if any did you experience as a result of your loss?

Ⓟ   From your earliest memory, trace your "death/loss" history. What impact has death/loss had in your life?

Chapter Two:
TABLE THE LABELS

Carolyn's Story:

When a person has a disability, especially one that is very visible, getting others to see us for who we are can be difficult. To be seen only in terms of a disability can be a source of intense grief. As someone with albinism, Carolyn has no pigmentation in her eyes, skin or hair. Having cotton white hair and very pale skin makes Carolyn very easy to notice. If that's *all* anyone notices, however, sadness, anger and frustration can result. Early on, Carolyn wanted to be "just one of the guys." The story which follows details her struggle to be seen as *Carolyn*, who also happens to be an albino.

I Wanna Be Me

"Everything is fine. We have a beautiful baby girl!" That's what my mom heard my dad say. The doctor was in the room and nodded his head in agreement. Then she drifted back to sleep (this was 1951, when mothers were given medication during/after the birth of their children, and fathers were not allowed in the delivery room).

The nurse brought me in at feeding time, and when she turned back the covers that surrounded my face and head, mom began to cry! What my dad and her doctor had failed to do was tell her that I was albino (no color in hair, skin, iris of the eyes; a genetic trait known well to our family). Mom didn't cry because of my disability. Her brother was an albino who was well on his way to a promising career in the education system. Her tears were those she'd known well, those of separation. She knew that I'd be leaving home at around age five in order to receive the education that it would take for me to survive. She knew this because she'd been through it before with her brother.

Mom told me that there were many more people who came to visit her after my birth than there had been after my sister was born. "Lookie Lous" she liked to call them, curiosity seekers who'd heard the news that there was something "different" about this baby.

I remember her telling me how my uncle had stressed to her the importance of making me as independent as possible, and how hard I'd struggle at something until I either got it, or she/my dad would save me after I became exhausted from frustration. Hey, my uncle's method worked!

My school years were wonderful. Everybody was blind or visually impaired and nobody felt labeled or "different." Nobody was "fat," "ugly," or any of those awful physical manifestations that can be cruelly put on children by other children. The only distinction I can remember us making was in saying what a rotten personality somebody had. I've often thought that, if the whole world was blind, there would be no prejudice! Many of our instructors were also blind or visually impaired. They made great role models for us because we realized that they'd been there and done that. It gave us a great sense of confidence and hope that we, too, could "make it" in the "real world."

I do remember an incident that clearly pointed to my being "different." Something had happened at the church in town that some of us would attend on Sunday mornings. Something about a bunch of us talking during the service. We'd been "turned in" to the school, and were called into the dean of students' office. I had the bright idea to ask her just "how" did she know that we'd been disrupting the church service. Her reply brought me up short. "You were identified by *your hair*. Anybody could spot you a mile away!" I was guilty, and I knew it, but it made me angry! For the first time, I realized that I wasn't and probably never would be "just one of the crowd." I remember answering her, "Well, I'll just wear a scarf next time!"

For the most part, I felt safe and secure in my world at school. It was really like a private education, with seven students per class and many extra curricular activities. My favorites were public speaking and traveling around the state with the folk group. I now use both of these skills in my personal and professional life. I work with Jeff to conduct workshops on grief and bereavement, and perform in a local "oldies" band.

Our instructors would warn us that life wouldn't be as accommodating once we left the protective walls that surrounded us. They stressed self-awareness and reliance, and worked hard to provide us with all that it would take to succeed "out in the real world," as they so aptly put it. We found it so hard to believe that things would be that different. How could we know just *how hard* it would be?

I got my *rude awakening* upon entering Lynchburg College, a private institution in central Virginia. I thought that I could be just like "one of the guys," already schooled in dorm life. I felt comfortable being in that type of environment. The administration had taken it upon themselves to notify my roommate of my visual impairment. You'd have thought that she had been told that I had the plague! She avoided me like I did, anyway.

Mealtime and going back and forth to my classes became a lesson in and of itself. There were some really cruel young "men," if you can call them that, who decided to begin a harassment campaign. They would shout, "white whale," every time they saw me anywhere on campus. They even went so far as to throw food at or on me in the dining hall. I called upon everything that I'd been taught. I figured that I'd better "get tough or die." I found myself taken in by a wonderful group of "rejects" that came to be known as the "Odd Squad." They were "outcasts," too, and I found my strength, my place among them. We began to be proud of our "difference," even flaunting it. They were, and still are, some of my best friends.

After I received my BA from Lynchburg College, I decided to get a Masters of Science at Virginia Commonwealth University, in Richmond, Virginia. These two schools were as *different as night and day*. My first few days at VCU were like a breath of fresh air. Richmond is a melting pot of all nationalities of people, and my albinism became a "point of interest." Edgar Winter (he and his brother, both albinos, were founding members of a famous rock band at that time) was extremely popular. People would walk along beside me as if I was his sister. Well, I guess we *are* related. It's all in the genes, you know. I had a friend from Egypt who told me that he had two albino brothers. He showed me their pictures. Darned if *they* didn't look like me, *too*! I guess that's why my Egyptian friend so readily accepted me. So, you see, an albino is an albino. It's kind of a universal thing!

I have often wondered just what color would I be if I had pigment. Would I be dark haired/eyed like my sister, or would I have been a strawberry redhead, with blue eyes, like my brother? I colored my hair red one time as an experiment. Actually, I put a weekly rinse on it. The hairdresser promised me that it would wash out if I didn't like it. *NOT!* I looked like Ronald McDonald, and after 40 washes, I still had a "pink tail" in the back for six months! When I looked in the mirror, I didn't recognize myself and hated what I saw. I wanted to put a bag over my head and be "unknown." Believe me, I'm well satisfied with being "cotton," as my cousin calls me.

I've had a lot of problems with people not knowing at first glance that I'm visually impaired. When I'm in stores trying to pick out cards, CD's and books, the store clerks always "point" to wherever the item I'm looking for is supposed to be. I've learned to ASK and to explain that I'll need some assistance. A blind person with a white cane and sunglasses is the CLASSIC stereotype of someone with a vision problem. Believe me, they would know right away that I had a vision problem if they followed me outside in the bright sun!

One time, during class at Lynchburg College, the professor was writing on the board, without saying what he was writing. I asked him to talk as he was writing. Some bright individual from the class hollered out, "What's the matter with you? Are you blind or something? Everything is on the board!" To everyone's shock, I stood up before the whole class and replied, "Yes, as a matter of fact, I am!" He shut up after that, and the professor made an extra effort to talk as he wrote.

I'd like to believe that people, for the most part, don't mean to be or act ignorant about persons with disabilities. Often it is so hard for them to "walk a mile in your shoes." How can they, if they've never experienced anything like it? My wish is that people could put themselves in the place of another person and realize the tremendous pain and hurt that is caused by thoughtlessness. It's like a sort of virtual reality.

I've found that, given the chance, the barriers against persons with disabilities can come down. Over the past 20 years there has been more positive press. I've taken every opportunity to educate others concerning my own disability. Much pain has been avoided by my own self-advocacy. I was fortunate that my "self-advocacy" training started early. My uncle, who is also an albino, told my mother to make me as independent as possible. He advised her not to do for me what I could do for myself and to teach me "when" to ask for help.

At the residential school I attended, I had many teachers who had visual impairments, or were completely blind. They helped me by sharing their own personal experiences. They frequently reminded me of the difficulties I would be facing when I left school. Using my visual impairment as an "excuse" didn't fly with my teachers. They had "been there" and "done that". I've been fortunate to have a "circle of friends" that accept me for who I am. They do not see me as a disability. I remember an incident when I was traveling with friends at work. It had been raining rather hard, and we were walking toward one of the buildings. I was walking slightly behind them. I noticed that they went to the left on the sidewalk, but I didn't know why until I had walked into the ankle deep puddle that my friends had swerved to avoid. They apologized profusely for not alerting me to the huge puddle's presence. Then, we all howled with laughter!

I've always been helped to believe, by my family, school, and very special mentors along the way, that I can do anything. Hey, I made my brother teach me how to drive, just so I could if there was an emergency and I might need to. I talked one of my cousins into "letting" me "pilot" his private plane (I only guided it up and down).

I enjoyed VCU and my ability to "fit in." I was studying Rehabilitation Counseling and many of my classmates had various disabilities, from leg amputation due to injuries received in the Vietnam War, to crippling arthritis. We were all there to learn how to help others with disabilities, but I think we ended up helping ourselves through our association with each other...the "wounded healer," if you will.

Keep in mind that in the 1970's, when I began looking for a job, it was "Pre-ADA" (Americans With Disabilities Act). I must have applied and been rejected for at least 20 jobs. When I was at Lynchburg College, I practically had to beg for my practicum. I went for an interview at the Local Sheltered Industries and was asked by their manager, "How many fingers do I have up?" He claimed that the question had to do with safety issues in the plant.

I also remember applying for a social worker position at the very place where I now work. The Director of Social Services was extremely "nice" at the interview, but later she wrote me a letter asking "How will you read or write? Social work takes a lot of paperwork." Again, I felt that old anger that had risen when the dean of students at my high school had awakened me to the fact that I was not anonymous. My reply to the Social Services Director went something like this (I didn't care at that point just what I said, since I was off to graduate school anyway). "It is obvious that I *read your letter*, and should be even more obvious, since I am *writing back* to you."

I had interviewed with Royal Smith, Unit Manager where I now work, three times. I felt good about the interview, but I felt that he still had misgivings about my ability to perform my duties as a team leader because of my visual impairment. I was desperate for a job! My father had died while I was in graduate school, leaving my mother and brother without support. They say that desperate men (or women, for that matter) do desperate things, so I decided to take the plunge. What did I have to lose? "Mr. Smith," I ventured, "you're black and I'm blind. I feel as if you know what it's like to have the doors of discrimination slammed in your face." "Ms. Bowling," he answered from somewhere very familiar to him, "do you still want this job? It's yours!" He rose from his desk and we shook hands, each seeming to understand where the other was coming from.

I've had some interesting things happen to me because of my albinism. I can get the "Senior Discount" (I'm not old enough yet) without having to be asked. Once, at the doctor's office, the doctor asked if the nurses could come in and look at me. He said, "Do you know how rare you are?" "Not in my family," was my reply, because there are quite a few of us. My cousin and I had this joke about the albinos in our family taking over the world. I had some kids from a local job corps circle me in the bus station. They were wondering if I was Dusty Rhodes, a famous wrestler at that time. I never said a word, and someone told me later that the kids came back telling the story of how they'd seen Dusty Rhodes in the bus station. I hooted!

God blessed me with a disability, which shaped my whole life. I may have had difficulty in seeing with my eyes, but I can see 20/20 with my heart. As for my wanting to be anonymous, well, that was a thing that I grew out of, developing instead, an abiding appreciation for who I am. I wanna be me.

Jeff's Story:

I was in the second grade. For some reason, I don't know why, my teacher came up to me and told me that I was stupid. Who was I to argue. After all, she was the teacher, the authority figure. I was sure that she must be right. Later in the year, when we took an intelligence test, I was never shown my score. In my mind, that confirmed that I was, indeed, stupid. I was certain that my teacher kept my score a secret because she didn't want me to know just how stupid I really was. Any hope I had of my teacher being incorrect was extinguished when she came to our home for a conference with my mother. She told my mother that I would never graduate from school. If I did, it would be after failing several grades. College would not be an option for me. My future was bleak. I remember thinking what a disappointment I must be to my parents. I wondered how they felt having such a stupid child for a son. For years afterwards, I did not apply myself in school as I could have. I figured that, since I was a stupid boy with no future, there was no point. My self image was significantly damaged.

It was lunchtime. I, and several of my seventh grade friends were on the grassy hill overlooking the football field. Suddenly, someone shoved me from behind and I went rolling down the hill, end over end. My glasses were broken. Without them, I had great difficulty seeing. Fortunately, I had an eye appointment in just a few days. I could make it till then. A couple of days before my appointment, my father dropped me off at the barber's for a haircut, while he ran a few errands. I sat down in a chair to wait my turn. The barber and his current customer eyed me curiously. Said the customer to the barber, "Look at his eyes. You reckon he's blind?"

Replied the barber, "Probably so. I'll bet he's retarded, too." I pretended not to hear, but I did, of course. His words cut as sharply as his scissors. The barber finished cutting the customer's hair, and the customer paid him. The barber looked at me uncertainly and said to the departing customer, "You reckon I should go over to him and offer to lead him to the chair?" The customer looked at me, shrugged his shoulders, and left the barber's shop. A white hot flame of anger grew within my chest. I'd show *him* who was blind and retarded! As the barber turned to attend to me, I was waiting quietly in the barber chair. The barber was completely speechless.

In college, I applied for several jobs, on campus. No one would hire me. "What if you fall?" "What if you get hurt?" "You're an insurance risk." "You'd be a liability." "Sorry. We need someone with experience." I wanted to scream, "How am I going to get *experience* if no one will take a *chance* on me!" It looked like my second grade teacher was going to be right. I had no future.

As a chaplain intern at North Carolina Baptist Hospital, in Winston-Salem, North Carolina, I spent six months as the chaplain for the Rehabilitation Unit. Patients there were in various stages of recovery from traumatic injury. One afternoon, a parent of one of the patients came up to me and said, "How nice that there is somewhere in this hospital for someone like you to work." I smiled and said, "Thank you." Inside, I was angry. I wanted to say, "My *place* in this hospital is anywhere I want to be!"

My internship was nearing its end, and I had yet to find a chaplain position at another hospital. Several of my fellow interns had gone to see the associational missionary, who often helped ministered find placements in area churches. I made an appointment to go see him.

The secretary told me that he was ready to see me. When I first opened the door to go in, he was smiling and coming toward me with his hand outstretched. As I walked into his office, he noticed my limp. The look of helpful friendliness instantly left his face. Though he still shook my hand, there was no warmth or firmness in it. While my fellow interns had all had interviews lasting at least an hour, mine lasted five minutes. There were no positions available for someone with my particular *profile*. A voice echoed in my head, "No future! No future! No future!" I wanted to cry.

I was walking in front of a local hospital. Two nurses were walking toward me. Being a friendly sort, I said, "Good morning, ladies." Looking at each other in astonishment, one said to the other, "Did you hear him? You could understand every word he said. He must be high functioning." I was taken aback. My smile faded. Why couldn't other people see me the way I saw myself?

On another day, I had just finished a worship service at a residence where several adults with developmental disabilities lived. As I was walking back to the church office, I happened to pass in front of the bus used by the residential staff. It was parked in front of the house. Staff and adults who lived there were getting off the bus and going inside to eat lunch. As I walked across the parking lot, a visitor stopped, got out of their car, walked up to the bus, and knocked on the door. "Excuse me," said the visitor, "but one of your people is getting away." Some people say that, "If it looks like a duck and quacks like a duck, then it must be a duck." Like the Cole Porter song says, "It ain't necessarily so!"

When I found out that I was going to work in Staff Development and Training, I was sharing with a friend my excitement at becoming a CPR instructor. "Don't try it," he advised. "Being an instructor is too physical for you. You'll never be able to complete the training." One year later, I was sent to Charlottesville, Virginia, along with my friend and co-worker, Randy, a recent addition to our department, to become an Instructor Trainer in CPR. We went to check in at our hotel. The man at the front desk handed us our room keys and, looking directly at me, said, "Sir, the *doors* to the rooms are numbered as well." Here was yet another person who seemed to think that if my leg limped, my mind must limp as well. The very next day, after successfully completing one of the CPR scenarios, my instructor exclaimed, "Wow! You did that almost as well as most *normal* people!" When she saw the look of surprise on my face, she apologized profusely. Even with her apology, her words still stung like a slap in the face.

The simple truth is, words *hurt*! They can slam into a person like a prize fighter's fist slams into an opponent's jaw, knocking him to the canvas. At least a boxer wears gloves, so the blow is somewhat softened. Thoughtless comments and purposefully derogatory remarks feel more like a bare knuckled brawl. While you may not be bleeding on the outside, on the inside your self-esteem is rapidly draining away.

Labels and preconceived ideas about a person can keep us from seeing someone as they really are, whether as family, business people, caregivers, or whoever. Anyone who has been victimized or limited by labeling can tell you just what kind of grief such experiences can cause. Labeling leads to prejudice, bigotry and victimization of others. Prejudice, in all of its forms is *wrong*! We must, myself included, do everything in our power to see one another for who we are. We must look past the labels and encourage people to show us who they are and to tell us what they need or want from us. We can only do this by building relationships with one another. To truly get to know someone is to learn to appreciate his or her uniqueness and diversity. I would like to share one final image.

One afternoon, I was sitting on the front steps watching my son, Ryan, play. He was about four years old. He stopped playing and came over to where I was sitting. It was obvious that there was something on his mind. "Daddy," he said, "how do you get secret paws?" "What?" I asked, confused. "You know. *Secret Paws*. Like what you got." "Oh," I replied, the light finally dawning, "you mean cerebral palsy. You get it when a certain part of your brain is damaged. Why do you want to know?" "Because I want it," came the surprising answer. "Why on earth do you want cerebral palsy?" I wanted to know. "Because you got it," he answered. I was struck with silent wonder. Ryan wanted to be like his daddy. He saw my cerebral palsy as simply a part of who I was...a cool part. Hopefully, there will come a day when we will all view each other through Ryan's eyes.

POINTS:

What Didn't Help:

➜ **Labels That Disable:** Within this one chapter, Jeff and I recognized the following labels: albino, different, visually impaired, white whale, odd squad, stupid, retarded, liability, high functioning and almost normal. How many did you come up with? Let's face it. It is human nature to label things and, *unfortunately*, people. Labeling *things* can be most helpful. No one would want to drink something marked "TOXIC." Labeling *people*, on the other hand, is fraught with difficulties. Being seen in terms of "the disability" one has can cause intense grief. (Being identified by my lack of hair color, "Anybody could spot *you* a mile away.") His second grade teacher labeled Jeff "stupid". Despite the support and encouragement he received at home, that label affected his self-esteem for years. Labels are necessary for identifying syndromes and medical conditions. However, when those same labels are attached to a person, that person tends to be reduced to that one aspect of his or her physical or personality make-up. None of us are one-dimensional beings. We are multi-faceted, complex individuals. No label is adequate to describe us. Even the well-intended label "disabled" falls far short of its intent to identify a certain group of human beings. Now that we think about it, there might be one label that's appropriate...our names. See us first as Carolyn and Jeff, etc. The rest will fall into place.

→ **Over Protection:** (Don't Over-wield the Desire to Shield.) My (Carolyn's) mother not being told by my father or her physician that I was an albino led to unnecessary upset for my mother. Because albinism is common in my family, my mother and father saw no shame in my condition. They grieved, instead, for the struggle they saw ahead for me. Others have no experience with disability. Over protection can lead to a sense of shame and self-blame, among other things. Jeff's friend was trying to protect him by trying to discourage him from becoming a CPR instructor because it was too physical. Fortunately, Jeff realized that if you never make the effort to achieve a goal, you never realize success. If we take the urge to protect too far, we may unintentionally send a message to the one(s) we seek to protect that they are incapable of coping with the situation.

→ **The Automatic "Teller":** Having someone else "pave the way" for me (Carolyn) by telling my roommate that I was visually impaired, instead of allowing me to tell her about my visual impairment myself, resulted in her avoiding me like I had the plague. If I had been allowed to speak to her on my own behalf, we might have become good friends *and* good roommates. Jeff was scheduled to take a CPR class for the first time. The instructor, not wanting to embarrass him, called his co-worker and asked if Jeff was able to kneel down on the floor. To his credit, Jeff's co-worker said, "Why don't you ask Jeff?" She did.

→ **Don't Be Cruel:** Labeling people as "different" in order to justify demeaning and humiliating them is simply inexcusable. There are cruel people in this world who harass those who are "different" from them. Carolyn was called "White Whale," and had food thrown at her in the dining hall at Lynchburg College. In school, I was known as that "crippled boy," and was hit, tripped and pushed down, resulting in my glasses being broken. Alex Haley was right. "You can never raise yourself by lowering another."

→ **Shooting From The Lip:** Many people engage their mouthpiece before enlisting their brain, thus leading to thoughtless words and actions, as in the incident at Lynchburg College when I (Carolyn) asked the professor to talk while he wrote on the blackboard and the student yelled out, "What's the matter? Are you blind or something?" Had the student taken the time to think before he spoke, he would have spared himself a great deal of embarrassment.

➡ *Nice*-tiness: The interview I (Carolyn) had for a social work position in which the interviewer was "nice" but then the interviewer rejected me without finding out how I would accomplish the tasks assigned to that job description, and Jeff's interview with the associational missionary to discuss employment options with area churches are examples of *nice*-tiness. Both interviewers were outwardly nice, but internally, they had both decided that we did not measure up. Had they engaged in open, honest dialogue, things might have turned out differently. If they had been truly *nice*, they would have been straight forward about their expectations and concerns, which would have given us the opportunity to share our goals, needs and abilities.

➡ **Lift the Curse From Being Diverse**: Being the smart reader that you are, I'm sure that you have figured out that labeling people in ways that casts their differences in a negative light is unacceptable. Individual differences and diversity are a reality of life. Simply being *human* is to be different. No two of us are exactly alike. Even identical twins are different because of diverse life experiences. It is well past the time to stop using differences to *separate* individuals and groups from one another. Instead, we must *celebrate* difference and diversity, which gives each of us our uniqueness.

Carolyn and I both feel that our disabilities have actually given our lives a texture and given us a perspective that has enriched who we are. In many ways, writing this book is a celebration of diversity. Sharing our stories enables us to show people with disabilities as three-dimensional human beings. People with disabilities need not be ashamed of their *difference*. We are *not* our disability. We are multi-faceted human beings.

When Jeff was told how fortunate he was to have a place in the hospital for *someone like him* to work, he *wanted* to say that his place was wherever he wanted to be, but he didn't. Now, however, when someone makes such a remark in ignorance, stupidity or meanness, he *does* speak up, not to offend, but to educate. When we respond to labeling with silence, we give the impression that we accept the label. If we are to change such unacceptable behavior, we must speak up! For those who cannot speak, we must be their voices. Caregivers, families and friends can educate their communities. It will help if we stop calling people by their disabilities. Let's call each other by our names! Let's build relationships. Let's celebrate one another's uniqueness.

What Did Help:

➜ **Two, Four, Six, Eight, Be A Good Self-Advocate:** I (Carolyn) have learned not to assume that everyone knows of my visual impairment at a glance and have become my own advocate in asking for assistance when needed. When I finally got up the nerve to make the statement to my future boss about his being black and my being blind and having the doors of discrimination slammed in our faces, I stepped out and took a chance, and it paid off. In addition to cerebral palsy, Jeff has arthritis, making it difficult to walk long distances. When he and a group of parents were going to take a group of cub scouts on a four-mile nature walk, he asked for a wheelchair. As a result, Jeff was able to enjoy the trip without pain. Jeff's willingness to ask for help is one example of how caregivers can foster self-advocacy in those they serve. We can model self-advocacy by asking for help when *we* need it. We can encourage those we help to help *us* when appropriate.

"It takes all kinds to make a world, big and little, men and women, boys and girls"...I think that's the way the song goes. Having a disability is simply another way of *being*. Teaching this truth is essential in helping people with disabilities to develop a healthy identity and a sense of pride in who they are. This is one of the first steps down the road to self-advocacy. "If I'm not for me, then who is?"

Caregivers can create an environment which encourages individuals with disabilities to explore issues involving prejudice, bigotry and ignorance. Fostering an atmosphere in which people are free to talk about how they feel when someone says or does something hurtful, whether out of mean spiritedness or ignorance, will enable them to gain perspective and self-confidence. It will also help them realize that, when people say or do hurtful things, it is that person's *attitude* that is at fault. Their disability is not to blame. Caregivers can also help those they serve to become aware of and to gain access to advocacy groups and community resources by inviting individuals from these groups to come and be guest speakers during group sessions, or by taking consumers to community forums and events where such issues are addressed. Caregivers can encourage involvement in advocacy groups, such as People First. Getting involved with area faith groups and volunteer agencies is also helpful.

Honest dialogue is essential. Caregivers can help people with disabilities take an honest look at their lives. Help those you serve take an objective look at where they are, where they want to be, and how to get there. Ask questions like, "What are your strengths? What qualities do you possess that make people want to know you? What do you like? What works best for you when you are going through a difficult time? What are your weaknesses? What qualities do you possess that get in the way of people getting to know you? What do you dislike? What does not work for you when you are going through a difficult time? What are your dreams? How can we help you to realize your dreams? What are five things that we can do right now to make life better?" This can be done with individuals, and in small group settings. When individuals have difficulty communicating likes or dislikes and other essentials, then family members, friends and caregivers can meet with the person and discuss these questions. The more that self-awareness is fostered in individuals with disabilities, the more self-advocacy will be developed.

The key to self-advocacy lies in fostering an environment that is both nurturing and empowering for people with disabilities. Caregivers are encouraged to: 1. Foster as much independence as possible. 2. Help individuals develop an awareness of their own strengths, while identifying barriers to their physical, emotional and spiritual growth and development. 3. Offer opportunities for choice making, whether simple or complex. 4. Encourage ongoing open discussions of prejudice and its affects on the individual. 5. Assure individuals with disabilities that someone else's attitude has nothing to do with their disability. 6. Help individuals establish a healthy self-image by pointing out their strengths and attributes and by point out positive role models, who also happen to have a disability. 7. Let people know that it's okay to ask for help by modeling this behavior yourself. 8.

Create connections with your community. Look for individuals, groups and community agencies that can enhance and expand the cool things that you are already.

➜ **"Roll Out The Role Models:** An uncle who had "been there/done that" encouraged my mother (Carolyn's) to make me as independent as possible. My school years at the Virginia School For The Deaf And The Blind were empowering, because faculty who were themselves visually impaired or blind mentored me, and served as role models. Seeing others like myself living fulfilling, independent lives fostered within me the realization that I, too, could achieve an independent lifestyle.

Caregivers can help those with whom they work to see the *coolness* of their disability by identifying *cool* role models with disabilities. Carolyn's picks for cool role models include: Stevie Wonder, Ronny Milsap and Ray Charles (all are musicians who happen to be blind). There's also Christopher Reeves (Superman), who has quadriplegia, due to receiving a spinal cord injury when he fell from his horse. He is now a film director and an advocate for persons with quadriplegia. Chris Burke, a young man with a developmental disability, played Corky on the television show "Life Goes On". Jeff added Jerry Jewel, a very funny comedienne and David Ring, a gifted evangelist. Both have cerebral palsy.

➜ **There's No Place Like Home:** A feeling of safety and security is essential for positive growth and development. Having a loving environment at home was a life saver. Home was my safety net, my secure haven. The world away from home, however, far too often left me (Jeff) feeling anything but safe and secure. The love and acceptance I received at home somewhat blunted the negative messages I got almost everywhere else. The love of my family helped to keep my hopes and dreams alive

→ **Walk A Mile In My Shoes:** The ability to put yourself in the place of another is an invaluable tool. Not everyone who does or says things that frustrate and anger us means to be callous or cruel. Often, the things they do and say come from their desire for us to achieve the best for ourselves. Putting ourselves in their place enables us to better deal with our frustrations and to better understand theirs.

→ **Ac-cent-u-ate The Positive:** Often, people in the "real world" who encounter people with disabilities put the emphasis on the *dis* of disability. We must help them look at the *ability*. Seeing ourselves as whole, complete individuals and projecting self-confidence is the first step. When others want to concentrate on what we *can't* do, we must emphasize what we *can* do. People who have never experienced disability sometimes have great difficulty imagining that a disability can have a positive side. Because of our disabilities, Carolyn and I have developed patience, empathy, tenacity, flexibility, creativity, a sense of humor, and other positive traits and abilities. Who wouldn't want co-workers and friends with qualities like those? (Did we mention humility?)

TOOLS YOU NEED FOR YOUR TOOL BOX

1. The ability to focus on the person rather than the disability
2. The willingness to tell the truth in a compassionate manner

3. The foresight to "back off" when your assistance is not needed
4. The ability to confront with compassion when someone is doing less for themselves than they are capable of doing
5. The patience and willingness to let someone show you what they are capable of doing
6. The courage to share your expectations and/or concerns honestly
7. A positive attitude that will encourage people to reach their highest potential
8. The ability to be quiet, enabling someone to tell their story in their way, in their time
9. The willingness and ability to model positive and appropriate skills, abilities and traits
10. The ability to teach appropriate skills and abilities which will enable someone to advocate for themselves as much as possible (and the willingness to be an advocate on someone's behalf when they cannot do so for themselves
11. The ability to call upon your memories of people and experiences in your life that have nurtured you
12. The ability to promote a sense of safety and security for yourself and those you care for
13. Knowledge of your own limitations and the ability to ask for help when you need it

POWER TOOLS

✪   Think about labels that you have given to other people. Why do you label them? How do you think they feel when you label them? How can you fight the urge to label others?

✦ Think of labels that others have given to you. How do you feel when you are labeled? How do you wish to be seen?

✦ Wear a blindfold and allow someone to be your sighted guide. Use crutches or a wheelchair for a day. Use headphones to significantly reduce your hearing. Bandage your dominant hand so that you cannot use it. What thoughts/feelings did you experience? How did you try to compensate for the sense or ability that was reduced or taken away? What frustrations did you experience? What positive feelings did you experience?

Chapter Three
DON'T REIGN ON SOMEONE'S PAIN

There are many types of loss other than by actual death. People face the loss of friends, pets, youth, property, jobs, abilities, and memory, to name a few.

With the publicity surrounding Hurricane Floyd a couple of years ago in North Carolina, and other national and international disasters, media coverage abounded, especially on television. This type of media focus calls for attention and funding for people who have suffered tremendous loss. Their grief is seen first hand. The Red Cross and other agencies send in "mental health counselors" to assist those who grieve both during and after the disaster. But what of the disabled? They are seldom "front page news," and are nearly always overlooked as persons who experience loss. What happens to those whose grief is not recognized, or to those who cannot openly express it?

The following stories help to illustrate different types of grief experienced by persons with developmental disabilities. They emphasize the importance of seeing each person as an individual, and in being creative in determining "what" and "how" a person grieves. These stories also illustrate the impact we can have on others by the types of intervention we implement.

In Lynn's case, she dreamed of marrying her boyfriend, Darrel. Circumstances at the time made the prospect of marriage unlikely. Though the dream of marrying Darrel was very real to Lynn, few took her seriously. Jeff and his co-workers, Jack and Priscilla, knew just how important Lynn's dream was to her, and they tried to be supportive. Jeff relates her story this way:

Lynn's Story

The first time that I encountered Lynn, she scared the living daylights out of me! I was sitting in the church secretary's office, waiting to be interviewed for a position as associate minister. My wife, Debbie, had come with me to check out the area. We were sitting on a sofa, talking with the secretary, Priscilla, while I waited for my interview.

As we were getting acquainted, Lynn came into the office. Lynn lived with several adult women with developmental disabilities in a residence near where I would be working. She helped out at the church. She swept, mopped the floors, and emptied trash cans. When she saw me, her face clouded over. Her eyes glowed with contempt. She reminded me of a hungry timber wolf who had just spotted dinner. Lynn said nothing. She just looked me up and down, and left the room.

Frankly, the silent encounter with Lynn had frightened me. "Who was that?" I asked Priscilla. "That's Lynn," she replied. "She helps out here during the week. She knows that we are interviewing for another associate minister, and she's not happy about it. She liked the one we had." "Oh," was all I said.

My interview went well, and I became the associate minister. My first Sunday there was a memorable one. It was time for the worship service, and I was standing at the front of the sanctuary with the senior minister, Jack. At least one hundred and fifty people had come to participate in worship. It was a lively service. Jack played the guitar, and we sang lots of hymns, gospel and contemporary songs. Jack introduced me to the crowd, and told them that I was the new associate minister. At the back of the sanctuary, Lynn stood up and pointed a finger at me. "You're not my minister," she yelled. "Jack is! *He's* my minister!"

After the service, I said to Jack, "My first Sunday here, and someone already hates me." He assured me that Lynn would come around. He said, "Lynn thinks that you've come here to replace me. As soon as she realizes that I'm not leaving, she'll calm down and learn to accept you." I certainly hoped that Jack was right.

Within a few weeks, Lynn *had* learned to accept me...even *like* me, and I had learned to accept and like her, too. If anyone came to the church and treated me in a manner that Lynn considered to be disrespectful, she let them know that such behavior would not be tolerated. Lynn had gone from hating my guts to being my fiercest defender.

Lynn had a boyfriend named Darrel. She loved him dearly. What she wanted more than anything in the world was to marry Darrel and live happily ever after, just like "normal" people. Often, as she was working, she would sing at the top of her lungs, "I'm going to marry Darrel Jenkins, oh glory!" When she wasn't singing about marrying Darrel, she was telling Jack, Priscilla or me about her plans to marry him someday. It was her one shining dream.

One day, Lynn, Priscilla and I were eating our lunches. We were sitting in the TV room watching part of "The Young and the Restless," while we ate. As fate would have it, during this particular episode, Nikki was marrying Victor Newman. Nikki was dressed in a beautiful wedding gown, and Victor was dressed in a tuxedo. They stared lovingly into each other's eyes as the minister led them through their vows. As he pronounced them man and wife, they embraced and shared a passionate, lingering kiss. It was the standard soap opera wedding.

As the ceremony ended and a commercial began, I heard someone crying. I looked up. It was Lynn. Hers were not the tears of someone crying over a tender moment shared. They were the tears of someone with a broken heart. With tears streaming down her face, Lynn said, "I want to marry Darrel!" Lynn knew that, unless she and Darrel could live independently, marriage wasn't likely. She hastily left the church, needing some time alone. Priscilla and I could only look at one another in silence, our hearts aching for Lynn and the pain that she was feeling.

Lynn helped me to see something that is very important, but often overlooked by those who care for people who have developmental disabilities and other disabilities. They have dreams, desires and hopes. In Lynn's case, she wanted something that most of us take for granted...to marry the person she loved, and to live with and be loved by that person for the rest of their lives together. Quite simply, she wanted the kind of life that she knew that Jack, Priscilla, and I had. Seeing Nikki and Victor exchange wedding vows together served as a painful reminder for Lynn of just how far she was from realizing her dream. If her dream was not dead, it was certainly badly bruised.

Priscilla and I grieved the unfairness of Lynn's situation. She wanted to marry Darrel, but was unable to do so because nameless, faceless people she knew nothing about had decided that Lynn, and others like her with developmental disabilities, were not marriage material. Rules, regulations, laws and policies make it nearly impossible for a man and a woman with developmental disabilities to become husband and wife. Making a "one law fits all" decision for people in a certain category is grossly unfair. I know many developmentally disabled people who would make wonderful spouses. By the same token, I know several "normal" people who should never marry. If you're honest, you do, too. Until society becomes more enlightened and learns to look at individuals rather than disabilities, we as caregivers must help those with developmental disabilities cope with the unfairness that life often throws at them.

Many of those with disabilities experience the significant grief that comes with the death or alteration of a cherished dream. Lynn grieved not being able to marry Darrel. Others I know grieve not being able to live on their own, not being able to father a child, not being able to drive a car or to hold down a full time job. The list is endless.

We as caregivers, parents, families and friends of people with disabilities must acknowledge the grief that they feel. We must be ready to give to them the same understanding and support that we require when we grieve a loss. When a person's dream must be abandoned, or reshaped, we must either help them to find the courage to dream a new dream, or we must learn to look at their dream through their eyes and find a way to look past our preconceived ideas of what is correct and acceptable, and find the flexibility to help them realize the dream they hold most dear.

Eventually, Lynn moved to a different place. Darrel had moved a year or so before. Often, when people move to a different place, they drift apart. Such was the case for Lynn and Darrel. Lynn, however, dared to dream a new dream. She dreamed of a home of her own. Happily, Lynn has realized that dream. She now lives in a new home and has begun a new chapter in her life. It is my hope that Darrel, too, has come to realize a dream of his own.

For all of the Lynns and Darrels of this world, I offer these few words to those who would dare to dream and to all who would help to make their dreams come true. This poem is inspired by John Lennon's song, "Imagine":

Imagine 2

Imagine lonely people,
Trapped deep inside themselves.
Imagine dreams, unspoken,
Stuck back on memory's shelves.
Imagine their eyes pleading
For something from ourselves.

Imagine people living
In places tucked away,
All living lives, well managed,
But they're allowed no say.
Imagine all those people
Existing day to day.

Imagine seeing people
Through love's unfiltered eye.
Imagine real acceptance.
It's easy, if you try.
Imagine all the people
Smiling 'neath the sky.

Imagine helping people

To realize a dream.
The task can be accomplished,
As hard as it might seem.
Imagine happy people,
Faces, all agleam.

Oh, some folks say I'm a dreamer,
But I'm not the only one.
I hope someday you'll help us
To make a place for everyone.

(Dedicated to Barbara Anne Clayton: A fearless dreamer and advocate for all who would seek to realize a dream of their own.)

Another need we would like to address is the need to have our feelings respected. Aretha Franklin was right: "R-E-S-P-E-C-T. Find out what it means to me." For people with disabilities, to be respected means a great deal...just as it does to every other person on the planet. I know that my friend, Linda, certainly needed and deserved some. Instead of respect, however, she almost got "The Needle."

The Needle

The phone rang. Linda's mother had died. Linda, a young woman with a developmental disability, was in the hospital, where I served as chaplain. The social worker asked if I would come and help break the news to Linda. I immediately went to the hospital, ready to give whatever support and comfort that I could. Knowing how special my own mother was to me, I could only imagine how I would feel if someone came to tell me that she was dead.

The social worker met me outside Linda's room. One of the nurses was with her. The three of us entered Linda's room. She was sitting quietly in a chair by her bed. Three other hospital patients shared her room. "We're really not sure how she's going to take the news," said the nurse. "I hope she doesn't get too upset. It would really make things difficult for the staff. Some of the other patients could get upset, too, and that would make for a long hard day for everyone. We really appreciate your coming over to break the news to Linda," she continued. "Glad to do it," I replied.

Linda was a soft-spoken, quiet woman. When she saw the three of us approaching her, she got up from her chair to meet us. By the look on her face, I could tell that she was wondering why the nurse, the social worker and I were coming to see her. "Hello, Linda," I said. How are you doing today?" "Okay," she answered softly. I took a deep breath. "Linda, I came to see you this morning because there is something I need to tell you." As I said this, I noticed that the social worker came to stand on one side of Linda, and the nurse came to stand on the other side. It was also then that I noticed the hypodermic needle that the nurse held in one hand, hidden behind her back.

I continued, "I'm sorry to have to tell you this, but your mother died yesterday." I watched Linda's face for a sign of emotion. There wasn't any. She remained calm. "Okay," she said. I told her, again, how sorry I was that her mother had died, asked if she would like to talk, and offered to sit with her for awhile. "No thank you," Linda said. "It's okay." She sat back down in her chair.

After we left Linda's room, I asked the nurse abut the hypodermic needle. "It was just a sedative to calm Linda down if she got upset," the nurse told me. "That way, she wouldn't bother the other patients and get *them* upset."

How strange, I thought. If Linda were not developmentally disabled, it would be seen as acceptable for her to get upset over the death of her mother. In this setting, however, the possibility of her getting upset was seen as a nuisance to be avoided, medicated. Thank goodness Linda had reacted *quietly*. She had been spared from the needle.

I am glad to say that I have never witnessed another scene like the one with Linda. I realize, of course, that, just because I haven't encountered a situation like that lately, it doesn't mean that such things no longer happen. They do. Fortunately, however, more and more people have come to realize that behavior has meaning...even behavior that is not convenient. Many people with very limited or non-existent verbal skills communicate primarily through behavior. We must respect their feelings, and their right to express them. Our task as family, friend or caregiver is to try and understand what a given behavior means. If we do that, we can find a way to support those we love and care for in a compassionate and respectful manner. Then, the Lindas of the world would be free to give expression to their grief, without fear of being silenced by the needle.

Society as a whole goes to great lengths to avoid pain, preferring to medicate it rather than deal with the underlying cause. We choose to suppress rather than to express our pain and discomfort. We often fear the possible reactions of the developmentally disabled to grief, bereavement and loss. The temptation to medicate is huge. Why should someone with a disability be seen as automatically needing "the needle"? There is no way to predict a person's reaction to loss, disabled or not. I have seen all kinds of reactions to grief from people with no known disability. Some can't walk. Some scream and throw themselves onto the person's coffin. Still others can't eat or sleep. Many develop psychosomatic illnesses. The list goes on and on. There is more than a little truth to the adage, "no pain, no gain". In fact, feminist psychology suggests that we cannot do our grief work if we are lost in a fog of prescription drugs or alcohol. At the most, the only thing accomplished by this kind of "pain management" is that the whole grief process is delayed. If we don't deal, we can't heal! If we are denied the opportunity to express our true feelings, we are destined to deal with our grief at a later time, perhaps in unhealthy ways.

In many ways, Carolyn and I are lucky. We were both born with our disabilities. We have never known a time when we were other than what we are. Carolyn and I have had a lifetime to adjust to, compensate for and become comfortable with our disabilities. Many people, however, become disabled after many years of normal life. They often experience a double grief. Not only do they grieve for what they were, they grieve what they have become. Sometimes, life goes into a tailspin as they struggle to rediscover who they are. They present a special challenge for those who seek to help them rebuild an identity as an intact person from the ashes of their former life. My friend, Phoenix, experienced this first hand.

Phoenix

I walked into the Burn Unit at North Carolina Baptist Hospital and greeted the staff. They were a wonderful group of caring professionals. Usually, they knew just what to do to best meet the needs of the burn victims who came to them. On this particular day, however, they were stumped. "We're glad you're here," they said. "We have a new patient in the corner room. He's one of the worst burn victims that we've ever seen. He won't talk to us, and he refuses to cooperate with us. Why don't you go talk to him and see what you can do? He calls himself Phoenix." I told them I would do my best.

I knocked on the door to Phoenix's room. Silence. The door was ajar, so I eased it open and went quietly into the room. It was almost completely dark. The only light came through the slits in the closed Venetian blinds. There was no sound, except for Phoenix breathing in and out. His breathing sounded somewhat ragged and labored. As my eyes adjusted to the dim light, I could see him lying in his hospital bed.

Phoenix was almost completely wrapped in bandages from head to toe. He looked just like the mummy in those B horror movies that used to scare me to death as a child and invade my dreams. "Phoenix," I said, almost in a whisper, "are you awake?" No answer. "Well," I said, more to myself than to anyone else, "I'll come back later." I turned around to leave. "Who are you?" a voice asked from behind me. Phoenix was awake.

His voice had startled me. I turned back toward the bandaged form lying in the bed. "My name is Jeff," I said. "I'm the chaplain. I wanted to meet you and introduce myself to you." Phoenix replied, "Come, sit down. I've been having bad dreams. They scare me. I'd like to talk about them." There was a chair by the bed. I sat down. "What do you dream about?" I asked. "Hell," he said. "I dream that I'm in Hell. I'm surrounded by flames, and I'm burning. It's so hot. I'm trapped, and I can't get out. Sometimes, I wake up screaming."

"Sounds like a scary dream," I said. "After what you've been through, I can understand why you might be dreaming that you're in Hell. Being burned must have been terrifying." My mind took me back to the day when I came very close to being seriously burned. I was in my college dorm room, frying French fries in a large frying pan, full of hot cooking oil, on my double burner hotplate. My dorm mates and I were having a fish fry. Several of my friends had gone to Atlantic Beach that weekend. The bluefish were running, and my buddies had caught several fish and brought them back in a big ice chest. I agreed to fry the fish and French fries. I had already finished frying the fish. Only the fries remained to be cooked.

I was sitting in a chair in front of the hotplate, tending to the French fries. Unexpectedly, a loaf of bread fell off of a shelf above my head and hit the frying pan, knocking the pan and the scalding cooking oil into my lap. I screamed in pain as the searing hot oil splashed into my lap, down my legs, and onto my chest and shoulders. At the same instant, cooking oil splashed onto the red hot burner of the hotplate. Flames shot up in front of my face, singeing my eyebrows, eyelashes, and hair. I was terrified. I thought for sure that I was going to die. I lurched back in my chair, trying to get my feet under me, so that I could get away from the flames. Oil on the floor made getting any traction difficult, but somehow I got away from the fire.

One of the guys in the room next to mine heard me scream. He ran into my room, grabbed me and put me in the shower. He made me stand in an ice cold shower for at least ten minutes. The water washed the oil off of my body, preventing it from further burning me. Thanks to my friend's quick thinking, I received only first and second degree burns. For the next week, I looked like the creature from the black lagoon, with bandages on my shoulders, wrists, legs and ankles. After that, I was fine. Thankfully, there was no scarring.

The flashback to my own experience of being burned lasted only a split second. I came back into the present. "How did you get burned?" I asked. "I was asleep," Phoenix said. "My girlfriend was mad at me. While I slept, she went into the kitchen, boiled a pot of coffee, put some red devil lye in it, came into the bedroom, and poured it on me. The lye ate the skin off my head and face, and blinded me."

I was horrified. Phoenix's description of what had happened to him almost made me physically ill. I could not imagine anyone being so angry that they would do something so vindictive. Phoenix was not finished telling his story. "I don't want to go to Hell," he said in a shaky voice. "What makes you think that you're going to Hell?" I asked. He continued. "I have not been a good person. I've been prejudiced and bigoted. I've hated black people. I used to belong to the Ku Klux Klan. I thought they were my friends, but they found out that I was part Indian, and they threw me out. They started treating me just as bad as they treated black people. I've been such a bad person that I'm afraid I'm going to Hell." Phoenix was on the verge of tears. We talked for awhile about how no one can change the past, but that the future was full of possibilities for building a different life. I left, excited that Phoenix and I had made a connection.

Over the next several weeks, Phoenix and I had many conversations. We got to know one another quite well. In the beginning, it was difficult for Phoenix to imagine a better future...or any future, for that matter. It was difficult for him to adjust to being blind, and the treatments for his burns were very painful. He was waiting to recover sufficiently for skin to be grafted to his head and face. He often seemed fearful and uncertain. Phoenix was convinced that he could not do even the simplest things for himself. He was almost totally dependent on the Burn Unit staff.

In the beginning, I would do small things for Phoenix. If he wanted a Kleenex, I'd get him one. If he wanted his milk, I'd hand it to him. If he needed to put something in the trashcan, I'd throw it away for him. Phoenix had reached the point where he *expected* to be waited on. He expected the same from the Burn Unit staff. We all realized that this could not continue. If Phoenix was going to have a life of his own, he was going to have to learn to do things for himself. We just had to remind him that he could.

The next day, I went to see Phoenix. It wasn't long before he started asking for things. "Give me my milk," he said. "No," I replied. "What do you mean, No," he asked, amazed that I had refused. "I mean," I said, "that if I do things for you that you can do for yourself, then you'll never learn to be independent. I won't always be here to get your milk for you. Besides, you can get it for yourself." "How can I get my milk, if I can't see where it is?" Phoenix asked. "Well," I replied, "think of your plate as the face of a clock. Your peas are at three o'clock, your potatoes are at six o'clock, and your pork chops are at nine o'clock. Your bread is at twelve o'clock, and your milk is beside your plate at about two o'clock. See if you can find your milk. Slowly, hesitantly, Phoenix reached out his hand. He found his mild, picked it up, and took a sip. A satisfied smile spread across his face. That was the beginning of his journey toward independence, and a new identity. Slowly, a new life would arise out of the ashes of the old.

Over the next few months, Phoenix had several skin grafts. He asked me to go with him into the operating room when the first operation was scheduled, because he was apprehensive. I went with him and stayed until I knew that he was asleep. After that, he didn't ask me to go with him anymore. Phoenix now knew what to expect, and was no longer afraid. His self-confidence continued to grow stronger. At long last, he was able to leave the hospital.

Even after I was no longer the chaplain for the Burn Unit, Phoenix would ask me to come visit whenever he came back to the hospital for another operation. He was adjusting well to his new life. When my year at North Carolina Baptist Hospital was over, I never saw Phoenix again. Even now, I think of him occasionally, and wonder where he is and how he's doing. Wherever he is, somehow I know he's doing just fine.

Phoenix was able to make a successful adjustment for several reasons. First, he was encouraged to grieve the parts of his life and his former self that he had lost. Also, we listened to his fears and acknowledged his pain. When he needed total care, he got it. As he required less, less was given. When Phoenix became too dependent on his caregivers, insisting that they do for him what he was capable of doing for himself, they set firm, but fair limits. Phoenix was not just set adrift to fend for himself. We explained to him what we would no longer do for him and why. We also helped him to attain the skills he needed to do things for himself. As a result, Phoenix became self-confident and, largely self-sufficient.

Phoenix's transformation from someone who saw himself as having no future to a person ready to live as full a life as possible did not happen over night. We worked with Phoenix over a six month period. Those adjusting to a disability, their families, friends and caregivers must be careful not to set unrealistic goals or expectations. Every person's situation is different. There is no one way to do a thing. Everyone involved in such a process would do well to employ the tools of clear, honest communication, active listening, compassion balanced with loving firmness when needed, and much patience. It may sound like an impossible "job description," but when you think about it, it's no more than most people in the world wish for and/or expect from the people in their lives.

THE POINTS

→   **You Irreplaceable You:** Lynn was initially angry because she thought that someone she cared about was being replaced. Positions can be filled with other people, but no one can ever truly be *replaced*. Never underestimate the power of the relationship. Lynn had developed a genuine affection for Jack. When she thought that he was being replaced, she was understandably angry. We must respect the feelings of those we care for, even the angry ones. With patience and understanding, we can help them learn to understand and cope with their feelings.

→   **Getting To Know You:** It is unrealistic to think that we will automatically be accepted by those we care for. We must first build a relationship of trust and mutual respect. Relationships take time. Don't rush it.

→   **Living "Not So" Happily Ever After:** People with disabilities experience loss other than death, as in the case of Lynn's unrealized dream to marry Darrel and live "happily ever after." People with developmental disabilities are often acutely aware of the near impossibility of their dream's ever being fulfilled (living on their own, holding a full-time job, driving, having a child), due to circumstances that are, many times, beyond their control. The rights of the disabled are often decided "by committee", leading to the denial of their civil rights as human beings. The grief for them is very real.

➡ **Activate...Agitate...Eradicate:** In order for a washing machine to work, you've got to turn it on. Once the washer fills with water, the agitator "stirs things up", freeing your clothes from dirt and grime. Self-advocacy groups for people with developmental disabilities must activate and agitate. We've got to stir things up and demand full citizenship for all people with disabilities, freeing them from unfair laws and policies. Only then will the dreams of people like Lynn and Darrel begin to be fully realized. There is enough grief that comes from disability itself. Those with disabilities do not need the added grief that comes from restrictions placed on them by others *because* of their disabilities. Come on! Let's get shakin'!

➡ **Don't Repeal the Right to Feel:** The nurse was all too ready to MEDICATE Linda, without having a clue as to her reaction to the news of her mother's death. The medication wasn't for Linda's sake, but to keep her quiet so that the other patients (or her caregivers) wouldn't be bothered or upset. If she had grieved more loudly, that might have made the day harder for everyone, especially the caregivers. Strong feelings are entirely appropriate when someone has lost a loved one. Trying to medicate such feelings away is _not_! If people are not encouraged to do their "Grief Work," unexpressed feelings will find expression through behavior, angry outbursts, depression, eating and/or sleeping disorders, etc., often for years. Many times, those in the medical profession still find it easier to MEDICATE rather than to make a commitment to PARTICIPATE in comforting and supporting those in grief situations, because writing a prescription is easier and takes much less time and effort. Grieving is a natural and necessary life experience. To deny the expression of grief is to rob someone of a part of his or her humanity.

→   **And You Were Expecting...?:** People don't always react the way that we expect them to. Such was the case with Linda. No two people express their grief in the same way. As caregivers, we must be careful not to make assumptions about how someone is going to react to a given situation. After all, you know what happens when we assume! Deciding in advance that Linda would need to be medicated was inappropriate and unnecessary.

→   **Self-Disclosure Or Over Exposure?:** Listening to Phoenix share his dream about being in Hell triggered Jeff's own memory of being burned in college. If Jeff had interrupted Phoenix in order to share his experience, Phoenix might have decided not to say any more. It can be tempting to share a similar experience in an attempt to show someone that we know how they feel. We don't. We only know how _we_ feel. While there is an appropriate time for self-disclosure, we must be patient enough to wait for it. We have two ears and one mouth. Listening twice as much as we talk is not a bad idea!

→ **From Sympathy To Empathy:** Jeff and the Burn Unit staff were constantly in touch with the fact that Phoenix had experienced a life changing event when he was severely burned and blinded as a result of domestic violence. When Jeff first met Phoenix, he worked on establishing rapport with him. He felt sympathy for Phoenix, remembering his own horrible experience of being burned. As time went on, that sympathy had to become empathy, so that Jeff and the Burn Unit staff could begin to assist Phoenix in grieving the loss of his former life and identity, enabling him to move toward a new sense of self, and as independent a life as possible.

→ **From Expectation To Motivation:** Honest communication, active listening, compassion balanced with loving firmness and much patience can be helpful in moving someone from expectation (when Phoenix began to expect Jeff and the staff to do for him), to motivation. Phoenix's self-confidence grew as he learned to do more and more for himself. His self-image of helplessness began to fade. He continued to receive emotional and practical support and encouragement from those around him for as long as he needed it.

TOOLS YOU NEED FOR YOUR TOOL BOX:

1. The courage to demand citizenship for all people with disabilities by forming alliances with self-advocacy groups wherever and whenever possible
2. The ability to acknowledge the dream, the dreamer and the grief a person feels when that dream dies or is altered
3. Creativity in helping a person develop the courage to dream a new dream

4. The willingness to look past your preconceived ideas of what is "correct" and "acceptable"
5. Flexibility in helping the person to realize (when appropriate and realistic) the dream they hold most dear
6. R-E-S-P-E-C-T for a person's feelings (do unto others as you would have them do unto you)
7. The willingness to participate in helping people express and cope with their grief, rather than medicating them into silence in order to prevent their grief work from being in constant re-runs
8. The ability to empathize, by calling on your own past similar experiences to help those you serve
9. The ability to empower the person to grieve the parts of their life, and/or their "Former Self" which has been lost
10. The willingness to acknowledge and listen to the person's expressions of fear and pain, and the willingness to feel it with them
11. The ability to set realistic goals for the person and for yourself
12. The patience to remember that *TRANSFORM-ATION* does not take place over night
13. The ability to wait for the appropriate time to share your own story
14. The patience to wait for a trusting relationship to develop between you and those you care for

POWER TOOLS:

- Think of a time when you had to give up a cherished dream. What thoughts and feelings did you experience? What kept you from being able to realize your dream? What might have helped you to make your dream a reality? What might you be able to do to help someone you care for to realize a dream that they have?

Chapter Four:
SURRENDAH YOUR AGENDA

Often, we have to let go of our "expectations" and experiences, and follow the lead of the individuals. In Jeff's telling of "Flora's Story," he illustrates how his own expectations as a young chaplain, fresh from the seminary, were changed by a group of people who refused to "grieve by the rules".

Flora's Story

I had only been working as a chaplain for a group of adults with developmental disabilities for a short period of time, when I received a call from their social worker. A woman in the residence, by the name of Flora Reese, had died, and the social worker was calling to ask if I would conduct a memorial service for Flora. It was a perfectly reasonable request. I was asked to conduct memorial services often. Little did I know just how different this one would be.

We agreed on a date and time for Flora's memorial service. Though I knew Flora, I didn't know her particularly well, so I asked the social worker to tell me some things about her that I could mention during the service. There was a moment of silence on the other end of the phone. Finally, the social worker said, "It's hard to come up with a happy memory of Flora." It was my turn to pause. "How sad," I thought, "not to have had one happy moment in her life." I could not imagine living a life without happiness or joy. "You can't think of one happy memory?" I asked. "No," she replied. "Flora just seemed to be miserable all the time. Nothing seemed to give her joy. She didn't like anything, or anybody. She seemed to go out of her way to make life difficult for everyone around her, housemates and staff alike. The staff tried really hard to find something that Flora liked or enjoyed. Nothing they tried worked with her. Just do the best you can. I'm sure you'll think of something."

For the next day and a half, the question of what to say about Flora was all I could think of. I asked staff who had worked with her for words of wisdom. They echoed what the social worker had said. "Flora didn't like anyone." I would just have to do the best I could. The time for her memorial service arrived. I read the most uplifting scriptures I could find. We prayed. We sang. During the eulogy, I remember saying, "Flora was consistent. You never had to wonder how she felt about you." No one could argue with *that*. I also talked about the fact that only God had truly known Flora's heart, and the reason for her misery. In conclusion, I said, "We can be glad that Flora has found peace at last."

Next came the part of the service where anyone who wished to could share a story about the person who had died, or just share their thoughts and feelings. Housemates and staff alike often looked forward to this part of the service. Many times, those who had lived with the deceased saw something positive in that person when no one else did. I was hoping that such would be the case now. One of Flora's housemates raised her hand and said, "I'm glad Flora's dead! I hated her!" Another hand. "I'm glad she's dead, too! She stole my lunch every day!" More hands. "She hit me on the head all the time!" "Flora was mean!" "I'm glad she's gone!"

I was in shock. This was not what I had expected. What had happened to my neatly planned memorial service? Just *when* had I lost control? I had hoped that at least *one* of the people who had lived with her had seen something likeable about Flora. No one had. Instead, they seemed relieved that she had died. In my mind's eye, I could see the Munchkins dancing merrily around the town square of Munchkin Land and singing, "Ding-dong, the witch is dead. Which old witch? The wicked witch! Ding-dong, the wicked witch is dead!"

After everyone had expressed their delight at Flora's demise, I thanked them for sharing, concluded the service (quickly), and made my exit. When I got back to my office, my mind was in a whirl. "What just happened?" "Was I really cut out to be a minister?" "Had I just proven myself to be a dismal failure?" "Would I ever be asked to do another memorial service or funeral again?" "What, if anything, could I learn from this experience?"

As it turned out, there was a great deal to be learned from the experience. Much of what I learned was about myself. One of the things that I learned about myself is that I can be a person of "shoulds" and "oughts." The biggest reason Flora's memorial service was such a shock to me is that, what my prior experience with death told me "should" happen, didn't happen. I had always believed that, when someone died, those left behind "should" be sorry. They "ought" to be sad. People "should" grieve. These things had not happened. Instead, people had been glad. People had been relieved. This "should not" happen. This felt *wrong*, and I felt that I had failed in my role as minister.

I also learned that I like feeling that I have things "under control." Too little control can lead to chaos. Too much control leads to rigidity and an inability to be flexible. Neither extreme is healthy. There needs to be a balance between the two. When Flora's memorial service took an unexpected turn, and people began sharing why they were glad she was dead, I felt most uncomfortable. My carefully planned service was not going the way that I had intended. Also, people were saying things about Flora that weren't nice. People "should" say positive things, or say nothing at all ("shouldn't" they?).

As I thought more about it, I realized several things. First, Flora's memorial service was not *my* service at all. The service was for those who had lived and worked with Flora. I was not there to "control" the service. I was there to provide an opportunity for people to express what Flora's life and death meant to *them*. By remaining silent and creating an environment encouraging those present to express themselves, even though doing so made me extremely uncomfortable, I had done that. For the people who had lived with Flora, the memorial service gave them an opportunity to celebrate the fact that they no longer had to live in fear of what Flora might do to them next. Second, I realized that death does not always lead to sadness for those left behind. Sometimes, death leads to relief, release, and a feeling of being set free. For me, those were lessons worth learning.

THE POINTS:

→ **Follow The Leader:** Whenever you enter a situation with your own expectations and "agenda," something is bound to go amiss, as with Jeff's "pre-conceived" notion about Flora's memorial service.

→ **What's Not To Like?:** Jeff had always been raised to believe that you should speak well of the dead. You know the old saying, "If you can't say something nice, don't say anything at all." The truth is that some people seem to go out of their way *not* to be liked. Flora, for whatever reason, was one of those people. As her housemates made crystal clear, sometimes, the best thing that you can say about someone is that they are *gone*.

→ **Who Stole My Control?:** Jeff had a real struggle trying to come up with something "nice" to say about Flora at her memorial service. All of his training had taught him that this was what was "expected" of him as a minister. He painstakingly crafted the service to be as *nice* as possible. As long as Jeff controlled the service, things went the way they were *supposed* to go. When, however, he asked Flora's housemates to share their thoughts and feelings, they took the service in their own direction, much to Jeff's shock and dismay, by openly expressing their dislike for Flora. Jeff left the service, certain that he had failed both Flora and her housemates.

→ **Taking From Our Mistakes:** Had Jeff failed to examine what had happened at Flora's service, he would have learned nothing. He would have continued to feel that he had failed as a minister. Instead, in looking at what had taken place, he realized that Flora's housemates had gotten what they needed...a chance to express their joy of being set free from the oppression of another. He was also able to examine and, where appropriate, change his expectations of himself and others. It is amazing what you can take from your mistakes.

→ **The Truth Shall Set You Free:** Though it was not his intent, Jeff provided Flora's housemates with an opportunity to express their true feelings. Being able to do so was very liberating for them. It was an invaluable lesson for Jeff.

TOOLS YOU NEED FOR YOUR TOOL BOX:

1. The courage to let go of your own expectations and to follow the lead of others
2. The ability to realize that it's OK for you not to like everybody
3. The ability to openly express your feelings and to foster an environment for others to openly express feelings about someone, whether positive or negative
4. The courage to go outside of your "comfort zone" and go with the flow (even when things flow in an unexpected direction)
5. The willingness to examine and to learn from your experiences
6. The willingness to give up being "in control"
7. The willingness to be silent and to empower others to express their true feelings (even when those expressions make you uncomfortable)
8. The ability to realize that a person's death does not always bring feelings of sadness or loss (it can bring a sense of relief, release, or freedom)

POWER TOOLS:

☸ Recall a situation in which things did not go the way that they were "supposed" to. What thoughts and feelings did you have? What could someone have said or done to help you in that situation? How did you cope with the situation? What did you learn from the situation?

"I have reached the conclusion that humor is vital in healing the problems of individuals, communities, and societies. People crave laughter as if it were an essential amino acid. When the woes of existence beset us, we urgently seek comic relief ... Humor is often denied in the adult world. Almost universally in the business, religious, medical and academic worlds, humor is denigrated and even condemned, except in speeches and anecdotes. The stress is on seriousness, with the implication that humor is inappropriate ... I insist that humor and fun (which is humor in action) are equal partners with love as key ingredients for a healthy life."

"Gesundheit"
Patch Adams, MD with
Maurine Mylander

I am reminded of an experience that I had when I was going to have some surgery. The "Patch Adams" method of using humor in the hospital was employed at a very stressful point for me. Because I'd passed out about a week before the surgery, and the reason wasn't clearly known, the anesthesiologists decided that it would be necessary to intubate (place the breathing tube down my throat), with me AWAKE! Just the sound of it scared me half to death! The two doctors could tell just how frightened I was by my talk with them, and by my vital signs in the operating room. They went to work, talking with each other and me as they did. One would say to the other, "She's freaking out on us. Give her a hundred cc's of...Ah, that did the trick." Then, the other doctor said to watch out for a certain artery as he passed the tube. "Oh, there she goes again," he'd say. "Just look at her blood pressure." Then, to me, "Now you know we have to have shop talk while we work." One played off the other, with humor, to try and alleviate my fears in a situation that none of us could avoid. I nicknamed them "Heckle and Jeckle." I don't think I could have tolerated that procedure without their humor.

I've experienced a long death history, which includes the murder of an aunt and uncle, three cousins killed by a drunk driver while they were walking along a country road, and my brother-in-law's long death following a self-inflicted gunshot wound, which was intended for my sister. Some people have compared the tragic experiences of our family to those of the Kennedy's.

None of these tragedies prepared me for what was to come. In 1986, my brother, Johnny, completed suicide at age 30, following many torturous years of mental illness. I wasn't sure if I would make it through the wake and funeral. I "went through the motions" like somebody wading through molasses while wearing lead boots that you can't take off.

Just at the time when I thought that I couldn't live through another minute of this horror, something came along to provide "comic relief." I know that the people around us must have thought my mother, sister and I were either very uncaring, or crazy. I'll share with you some of the humorous things that "got me through" my brother's wake and funeral, and helped me to begin to realize that life truly would go on.

Johnny would have really appreciated some of the humorous things that happened after his death. Our family is a large one, and it seemed to me that everybody that was somebody showed up for his "viewing." Johnny hated crowds, and I told my mother that he would be "making a new door," a phrase he repeated many times in his life, which described his need for space. His grave is on a hillside, so, during the graveside part of the funeral, we were seated downhill, with my mom first, my sister second, me next, and then Carroll, my nephew. He was almost ten at the time. I must tell you that we are not small women. My mom whispered to my sister, who whispered to me that if she tumbled over, then my sister, then me, Carroll would be squashed. The preacher decided he was going to save all the unsaved, and ended up giving his phone number. All I could think of was, "For a good time, call BR-549," from the old TV show, Hee Haw.

When I asked Jeff about a stressful situation he recalled, he reminded me of a memorial service in which the person was cremated. Jeff had never conducted a ceremony in which the ashes had to be scattered! In fact, he had never seen someone's cremains. He was expecting the funeral home to deliver the ashes in an urn. Instead, he was given a cardboard box. The ashes were in two plastic bags, closed with twist ties. He did not feel that he could scatter the ashes from the plastic bag. He thought that it would look like he was "feeding chickens" if he scattered the ashes that way. With no urn, he wondered how he could scatter the ashes in a dignified manner. Rummaging around in the basement of the chapel, trying to find something "appropriate," his mind was filled with uncertainty and concern in this unfamiliar situation. His mind soon began to do funny things to him as he searched for a container for the ashes.. A nonsense poem formed in his mind. "Ashes to ashes. Dust to dust. If you'd have been metal, you'd be rust." That made him laugh, and eased his tension, allowing him to focus on the task at hand. He found a wicker flower basket, knocked the dirt out of it, and put one of the plastic bags full of ashes down in the basket. The bag could not be seen, and the basket looked much more dignified. Everything went just fine, until everyone arrived at the cemetery and the time came to scatter the ashes. As he began to scatter the ashes, the wind changed direction, blowing ashes back onto his pants. He said he took some of the departed home with him in his pant cuffs. Being able to see the humor in the situation broke the tension and allowed Jeff to do what he needed to do.

If you have ever been to a rodeo, you have no doubt been amused by the antics of the rodeo clown. The first time I watched a rodeo clown cavorting around the arena, I thought that he seemed very much "out of place." Clowns and rodeos just didn't seem to mix. He was very amusing, but why was he there? As I watched him go through his routine, I began to understand his purpose. He only appeared when a cowboy was in danger of being trampled or gored by an angry bull. By waving his hat and running around barrels, he distracted the two thousand pounds of moving sirloin, giving the endangered rodeo rider a chance to run to safety. This was humor with a purpose.

Humor in the midst of grief, or a stressful situation can be very appropriate. Someone has said that laughter is God's hand on the shoulder of a troubled world. Jeff and I are in agreement with that statement. You have probably noticed that humor is sprinkled through many of our stories. It often eases some of the tension or stress of the situations in which we find ourselves. The next time you find yourself in a difficult spot, remember the rodeo clown. Laughter can, indeed, be the best medicine.

THE POINTS:

→ **It's No Laughing Matter:** Humor is often denied...especially in the "adult" world, and is often completely overlooked in the world of the disabled. During a time of grief or loss, many people see humor as inappropriate.

→ **Oh, What A Comic Relief It Is:** Humor often comes during the most stressful times in a person's life. I (Carolyn) gave the example of having to have a breathing tube placed down my throat, while awake. Jeff told the story of his first funeral service, which involved dealing with a person's cremains. In both examples, we were faced with the stress of the "unfamiliar." Humor provided us with a "release valve," which helped to reduce our stress and allow us to cope with our situations.

→ **Send In The Clowns:** When faced with my brother's death from suicide, I thought I would never make it through. Like the rodeo clown, coming to the aide of the endangered cowboy, humor provided the comic relief, which helped me begin to realize that life would go on.

TOOLS YOU NEED FOR YOUR TOOL BOX:

1.   The realization that humor can be "appropriate" during times of extreme stress

2.   The ability to recognize the difference between appropriate and inappropriate humor
3.   The ability to help those who see humor in the midst of a horrible situation to realize that they are not "crazy" or "uncaring"
4.   The compassion not to use humor at the expense of someone else
5.   The ability to laugh *at* yourself and *with* others
6.   the wisdom to know when to laugh internally and when to laugh externally

POWER TOOLS:

☥   Remember a stressful situation in which you used humor to relieve the tension. How was humor helpful?

☥   Recall a situation in which humor was used inappropriately. How did inappropriate humor affect the situation?

Chapter Six
CARE GIVING & CARE TAKING

"Walking with your loved one on the journey to the edge of the physical life is stressful, painful, and perhaps one of the most difficult and rewarding adventures you may ever have. It is an honor and privilege to enter the most intimate moments of another's existence, knowing that it is a moment of oneness with all that is. It is a walking together to the final destination where time stands still and expands to allow the ceasing of a heartbeat and the freeing of the spirit."

"Practical Wisdom For The Dying & Their Caregivers"
Joan Furman, M.S.N. and David McNabb

The above quote does an excellent job of summarizing Jeff's and my thoughts and attitudes on caregiving. We are all caregivers at some point in our lives. We will all be faced with grief, bereavement and loss. Knowing this, we need to acquire the tools necessary to give compassionate and appropriate care to those we serve and care for. We hope that you have already discovered several useful tools within this book. In this final chapter, Jeff and I wish to address caregiving specifically.

This topic is divided into several chapters. Each chapter will address one aspect of caregiving. First, we will look at caregiving without compassion and care giving with compassion. Next, we will touch on the role of the caregiver. Another issue to be addressed is the importance of asking for help when you need it. The necessity of acknowledging that, sometimes, even our best efforts to give care are not enough will also be examined. Finally,

Jeff and I wish to share some "snapshots" of individualized caregiving.

From Compassionless To Compassionate Care

"I got needs, you got needs, all God's children got needs," to give an old song a new twist. Everyone has needs. That's certainly nothing new. Sometimes, however, we simply need to be reminded that there are certain attributes necessary to be an effective caregiver for a person with disabilities...or anyone else, for that matter. These same things are essential to be the best possible parent, family member or friend. We sometimes realize what we need when we don't get it. In the story that follows, my number one need was for compassion from a caregiver.

The Nun's Tale

When I was ten years old, I had the first of two heel cord operations on my right heel. Cerebral palsy caused me to walk on my tiptoes, like a clumsy ballerina. Hopefully, heel cord surgery would correct that. The operation took place in a small, Catholic hospital, where the nurses also happened to be nuns. I had undergone a few other surgeries when I was younger, so being in the hospital was not a new experience for me. No one, however, had prepared me for just how painful such an operation would be.

     Whenever I had been in the hospital before, my mother's face was always the last face I saw as I was wheeled out of my room to go to surgery. She was also the first person I saw when I got back to my room. She was my security in a strange place full of unfamiliar faces. The morning of my heel cord surgery, there she was, smiling her smile of encouragement and comfort, as I was taken out of my room for surgery. With mother there, I knew that everything would be all right.

In the operating room, a doctor, with a mask over his nose and mouth that made him look like Jesse James, put a mask with ether over my nose. He asked me to count backwards from 10. As I began to count, darkness overcame me. I was asleep. When I woke up, I was back in my room. Something wasn't right. My mother wasn't there. Her absence frightened me. In the same instant that I realized my mother was gone, I felt a searing pain in my right heel. The pain was so intense, that it caused my right leg to spasm. I could not straighten my right leg. It hurt so badly! I began to cry. I simply couldn't help it.

As I began to cry, a nun/nurse entered my room. I was so relieved that someone had come to comfort me. "She'll help me," I thought. "She'll know where my mother is, and she'll be able to make this horrible pain better." After all, even I knew, at the tender age of ten, that all nuns were nice. That nun in "The Sound of Music" had been wonderful. She had sung such happy songs. I was hopeful.

Hope was short lived. There was no smile of comfort on her face. There was no kindness in her eyes. The nun/nurse spoke. "Why are you crying? Big boys don't cry! Why is your leg up like that? That leg is supposed to be straight! If that leg isn't straightened out the next time I come into this room, I'm going to sit on it!" Without another word, she turned and left the room. I was sick with fright! As bad as the pain already was, I could not imagine how bad it would be if the nun/nurse came back and sat on my leg. I was scared to death!

Soon after she had left, my mother came into the room. I had never been so glad to see anyone in my life! I felt safe and secure. I could allow myself to sleep a little...until I thought of the nun coming back into my room and sitting on my leg. I had to straighten that leg out. I just had to!

It took several hours to straighten my right leg out. In the beginning, it seemed that I would straighten my leg a couple of inches, only to have another spasm erase most of my hard work. Watching TV helped to take my mind off of my painfully cramped leg. Little by little...inch by inch, my leg finally straightened out completely. I was safe! The nun/nurse wouldn't have to sit on my leg. For the first time all day, I could sleep without fear.

The multiple hospitalizations that I experienced growing up played a large role in my becoming a chaplain. This particular experience fueled that desire more that all the others. When I first realized that I wanted to go into a helping profession, I knew that I wanted to do all I could to make sure that no one would have to lay in a hospital bed, alone, and be frightened to death. Having felt first hand what it is like to be treated with no compassion made me want to be as compassionate as possible. I might not be able to make someone's fear and apprehension magically disappear, but I *could* understand it.

My experience with the nun/nurse made one truth perfectly clear to me. Functioning in the role of caregiver does not guarantee compassion and understanding. My assumption that she must be nice because she was a nun was clearly wrong, just as it is wrong to assume any person in a particular group *must* behave in a certain way. We are all individuals. We carry our own baggage with us. Compassion and understanding in helping professionals is not a given.

In her defense, I can say that she probably thought that how she handled the situation was in my best interest. Tough love, if you will. After all, threatening to sit on my leg got her the results she wanted. I did work very hard to straighten my right leg. To me, however, fear and dread were a high price to pay for success. If the nun/nurse had simply taken a moment to understand and acknowledge my feelings and explain the importance of working to straighten my leg, she would still have gotten the results she wanted, and I would have gotten a lot more rest.

Sometimes, due to physical or mental illness, people can become lost within themselves. It is difficult to care for someone who is adrift on a sea of confusion, seemingly cut away from his or her mental moorings. A very wise friend of mine once told me that whenever she found herself caught within the whirlpool of crisis and confusion, she looked within herself to find a core value or belief to cling to...something that gave her life real meaning. She compared such a situation with being adrift on the ocean when your boat has been sunk by angry waves. In desperation, you look around for anything from the shipwreck that you can cling to in order to survive. Put simply, you cling to what floats. There are times when people just need something to cling to, and the best that we can do is to try and help them find that *something*. I'd like to illustrate my point with Rolfe's story.

Rolfe's Story

I was visiting the patients and staff on the hospital one afternoon. As I turned the corner to go to the nurse's station, there sat Rolfe. He sat in a chair with a tray board attached to it, without a stitch of clothing on. He was obviously very agitated and restless. The air conditioner was on and it was quite chilly, so the staff were trying to convince Rolfe to put on a T shirt and some shorts. Rolfe was loudly refusing. It was difficult seeing him this way. As his physical illness progressed, he was losing his grasp on reality and retreating into some interior world of the mind where we could not follow.

Twelve years earlier, Rolfe had appeared at the church door wanting a cup of coffee. He lived in a nearby residence, with several other men who were, like Rolfe, developmentally disabled. Coffee was one of his passions. He had short, close cropped hair, and thick, Coke bottle glasses in black frames. He talked slowly and deliberately, in his quiet way. "Give me a cup of coffee," he said. "Okay," I replied, and handed him a cup. Rolfe began gulping the cup of coffee, as if he was afraid that someone might take it away from him. "I want two cups," he said. I told him that, for dietary reasons, I could only give him one cup of coffee in the morning, and another cup in the afternoon. Rolfe came back that afternoon for his second cup. After that, he came every day, once in the morning, and once in the afternoon. He was a faithful patron.

So great was Rolfe's love of coffee that it sometimes led to conflict. Sometimes, during Sunday morning worship, Rolfe would come up to me right in the middle of the service. He'd get right in my face, staring intently at me through his thick, Coke bottle glasses and ask, "You got any coffee?" "No," I'd reply. "We're having worship service now. I didn't make any coffee this morning. You'll have to come back tomorrow morning for coffee." Rolfe would glare at me and say, "You don't got any coffee? Then I ain't coming back to this church no more!"

Then, he would turn, stomp down the aisle and storm out of the door. I would not see him for the rest of the day. Bright and early Monday morning, however, he would again appear for his coffee.

As much as Rolfe loved coffee, there was something that he loved more...cars. Almost every time that Rolfe came to see me, he would ask, "What kind of car you got?" I'd tell him what kind of car I had, and he would reply, "When you going to get a new car?" "I don't know," I'd answer. "What kind of car do you think I should get?" "I like Ford cars," he'd say. "Well," I'd say, "I'll keep that in mind when I'm ready to buy a new one." Came Rolfe's reply, "Okay. I'll see you tomorrow." And so went our dialogue for several years.

And now, here was Rolfe, naked, confused, upset, and lost in a mental no man's land. My heart ached for him. An idea flashed into my head. "Hey, Rolfe," I said. "I'm thinking about buying a new car. What kind of car do you think I should get?" Rolfe stopped his protests. A light of recognition came into his eyes. "You thinkin' about getting a new car?" he asked. "Yes," I said. "What kind of car you got now?" came the question. "A Plymouth Sundance," I answered. "Get a Ford car," Rolfe said. "I like Ford cars." "I'll think about it," I promised. He smiled, pleased that I had asked his opinion. He was calm now and happy.

"Hey, Rolfe," said one of the nursing staff standing there with me, "How about putting on this T shirt and some shorts so that you won't catch cold." "Can I have a Coca-Cola?" he asked hopefully. "I'll get it for you right new," she replied. When I left, Rolfe was sitting in his chair, wearing a T shirt and shorts, and enjoying his

Coke.

Sadly, Rolfe died soon after that. It gives me comfort to know that, for one brief moment in time, I was able to give him a plank of remembrance to cling to amidst the sea of mental confusion in which he struggled. It also makes me happy to think that Rolfe might occasionally look down from heaven to see what I'm doing. If he does, I know that he must surely smile a satisfied smile to see me driving around in my black Ford Escort.

THE POINTS:

➡ **Someone To Watch Over Me:** Jeff was frightened when he returned from the operating room and found that his mother was not in the room waiting for him. In the past, he had always found security in her presence. He had come to depend on her always being there. No one can *always* be there, but as caregivers, we want to provide as secure an environments we can for those who count on us.

➡ **Where's Julie Andrews When You Need Her?:** Jeff expected the nun who came to his room to be like the ones he had seen in the movies and on TV. He thought that she would comfort him in the midst of his fright and pain. Unfortunately, real life is often far removed from what we see on the large and small screen. When it is necessary for someone to receive care in an unfamiliar environment, we as caregivers can help by preparing them for what they are likely to experience.

➡ **Ban The Bully:** Not everyone inhabiting the role

of caregiver should be. Some people in that role use it to make themselves feel powerful, and to exercise control over others. This is abuse, and NEVER to be tolerated.

➜ **Ain't No Guarantee:** Functioning in the "role" of caregiver does not guarantee compassion and understanding. The nun's lack of compassion showed Jeff how necessary it was to have empathy for those who suffer, and to be an example for those who provide their care.

➜ **Pain Can Bring Gain:** The multiple hospitalizations and pain that Jeff experienced in his early years helped to shape his desire to help others by becoming a chaplain.

➜ **Throw Me A Life Line:** Jeff was heartbroken to see his friend, Rolfe drowning in a sea of confusion and fear. Because he had a relationship with Rolfe that spanned several years, Jeff was able to make a connection with him. Jeff called on his memories of Rolfe's love of cars to break through Rolfe's confusion and help him begin to calm down.

TOOLS YOU NEED FOR YOUR TOOL BOX:

1. Compassion
2. Empathy
3. The patience/willingness to develop a relationship with those we care for
4. The ability to provide a sense of security for someone if they are frightened
5. the courage to advocate for someone who may have an abusive caregiver
6. The ability to prepare someone for what they

might experience

7.   The ability to draw from your own experiences to help others

POWER TOOLS:

⊛   Recall a time when you needed comfort and assurance but didn't get it. How did you feel? What do you wish had happened? How can you use your experience to help someone you care for?

⊛   Recall a time when you got the comfort and assurance that you needed. How did you feel? What characteristics of your caregiver would you like to develop within yourself. How can you develop these characteristics?

⊛   Do a role play based on Jeff's experience with the nun/nurse. Discuss thoughts and feelings experienced through the role play.

Chapter Seven

PUTTING THE "GOOD" IN GOOD-BYE

We are as emotionally affected by the people close to us, as they are by us. Our role as caregiver is very important to the people we serve. We often have no idea how a person is going to react to loss, such as the loss of a caregiver. In fact, their reactions are often a complete surprise to us, as was the case with Marianne.

Marianne's Story

In the summer of 1978, I worked as a ministry student in Louisville, Kentucky. I was enrolled in the Clinical Pastoral Education program, and would be working with people who had some form of mental illness, or disability. Having majored in Psychology in college, I was looking forward to the experience that I would gain in such a setting. There were at least seven other ministry students present on the first day of orientation. As we were getting acquainted with one another, one of our CPE supervisors announced that the student who was to have been assigned to a group of adults with developmental disabilities had dropped out of the program. Someone was needed to serve as their student minister for the summer.

Because I was the only one who completed a previous unit of CPE, it was decided that I would become their student minister. Several developmentally disabled individuals lived together in a residence. I would be with them for the next ten weeks. Having never worked with people who were developmentally disabled before, I had no idea what to expect. The resident manager had scheduled a meeting with me that afternoon. I figured that I would have a better understanding of what to expect after talking with her.

The resident manager was very cordial. She asked me why I wanted to work with the developmentally disabled. I was honest with her and explained to her that I had no previous experience working with developmentally disabled individuals. I also explained that I had been assigned to serve as their minister because I had more CPE experience than any of the other students, and that I was willing to give it a try. I was not expecting what came next.

The resident manager was wearing a turtle neck blouse. She pulled down the collar to reveal a small scar on her neck. "Do you see that scar?" she asked. I nodded. "I got that when Minnie tried to choke me." She next pulled up the pants leg on her right leg to reveal a half moon scar. "I got that when Jewel bit me." She showed me another scar on her knee that she got when Sonnie cut her with a knife. She shared stories of other staff with broken glasses, broken bones, and assorted other injuries. When she had at last finished trying to scare me to death, she gave me a penetrating look and asked, "Well, do you still want to work here?" "Yes, I do," was all I said. "Well, then," came the reply, "I have one piece of advice for you. Whenever you sit down, make sure that you sit with your back against a wall so that no one can sneak up behind you and hurt you."

Armed with that bit of sage advice, and a healthy dose of apprehension, I went forth to meet the people for whom I would serve as minister. There was Jewel, whose major concern was when she could have her next cigarette. Minnie took great pride in her work at the vocational workshop where she was employed. She patiently showed me how to put the anchor caps on concrete nails. Nettie loved her doll, and carried it with her wherever she went. Sonnie liked oatmeal cream pies, and listening to the train whistle as the train rumbled down the nearby track. Katy spent most of her time trying to get the other residents to do her work for her, like a female Tom Sawyer. Ellen had a dislike of clothing, and was often trying to disrobe.

And then, there was Marianne. She was the quiet one, and rarely spoke. It would have been easy to forget that she was there. But there were her eyes. They caught your attention. Marianne had the biggest, most expressive brown eyes that I have ever seen. All of her emotions were conveyed through her eyes. Often, they seemed to register a great inner sadness. I made a special effort to speak to her whenever I saw her. I wanted to make a connection somehow. I wanted Marianne to know that I knew she existed. If I made any kind of impression at all, it did not register on Marianne's face.

By the end of the first week, I had stopped sitting with my back to the wall. My favorite day of the week became Sunday. I thoroughly enjoyed our worship services. They were held in the laundry room. Most of the time, as we sang and prayed, there was a load of clothes going in the washer, and another load going in the dryer. Often the buzzer on the dryer would go off in the middle of my brief sermonette. If the buzzer didn't get me, Jewel would let me know that she was ready for a cigarette.

The weeks passed quickly. Before I knew it, my time with my small flock was almost up. At least two weeks before I was to leave, I began talking to my parishioners about having to go back to school, and my not being able to be with them anymore. For the most part, they took the news well. After all, they were used to

CPE students coming and going. That's the way things were.

And then, there was Marianne. I will never forget the day I told her that I would be leaving. I said, "Marianne, I won't be here much longer. I'll be leaving in two weeks to go back to school. I have really enjoyed being here this summer." I expected no response, but, to my surprise, Marianne replied, "You are leaving? I will miss you." And in those big, expressive brown eyes, large, wet, glistening tears welled up and spilled over. She gave me a hug, and she was gone.

Marianne taught me, in her quiet way, that we never truly know just how much or how deeply we touch the people with whom we work. People may come and go in their lives in a seemingly endless stream, but each is unique. We can and do touch lives in profound, yet subtle ways. We do, often make a difference, and when we leave, there is often grief at our departure. We do well to acknowledge such feelings and to give what comfort we can.

THE POINTS:

→ **From Apprehension To Comprehension:** Jeff's first experience working with people with developmental disabilities began with the resident manager doing her best to scare the wits out of him. For the first six months of my job serving people with disabilities, I promised myself each day that I would not go back. I'm glad that I did not keep that promise. With each passing day and every new experience, *family*-arity grows. It is normal to be apprehensive when you work with unfamiliar people in unfamiliar surroundings. There's a first time for everything. Many of us come into our jobs with little or no experience working with people with disabilities. Fear, sadness and helplessness are just a few of the emotions we may experience. Remember that fear is energy. You can allow fear to freeze you into inactivity, or you can see it as a challenge to rise above. The choice is yours.

→ **Form Your Own Opinions:** So, many times, the negative pictures that others paint for us make lasting impressions on us. We tend to base our opinions of people on what has been said, or we look for behaviors that have been described. Jeff took time to get to know each person and make his own observations. He found something special in each individual. He wanted to make a connection with each person, especially Marianne, "the quiet one." He wanted her to know that he saw her as a special person and that she mattered.

→ **Lasting Reflections Through Making Connections:** The connection Jeff made with Marianne was evidenced by her tears when he told her that he would be leaving and returning to school. Though Jeff had made a point to speak to Marianne each time he saw her, she made no response that he could see. Internally, however, Marianne registered each encounter. Jeff made a lasting reflection of himself in the mirror of her innermost self. I met someone that I had not seen for eight years. I had been one of his caregivers. he recognized me immediately. We may not know what effect our care has on others because they may not be able to openly express their feelings. Don't be discouraged if a connection is not immediately apparent. Simply continue to affirm and support the individual. Keep in mind that we often touch people's lives in profound, yet subtle ways that we may never realize.

Also, many of the people we serve have numerous caregivers and many different living situations. They may have become desensitized to caregivers entering and leaving their lives. This may be a defense to keep from being hurt when someone you grow to care for leaves. Imagine how you would feel if this happened to you time and time again.

Patience and consistency help to build an atmosphere of safety, security and trust. I found this out firsthand when our band was playing for a dance sponsored by the local community service board. I knew that the residents from a home nearby would be coming. One of them was a fellow I'd served about 20 years ago. He was a real joy to be around. When I first met him, he'd burst into my office, making all kinds of noise (he is deaf). He soon learned to knock gently on my office door. If I was on the telephone, he'd put his index finger to his mouth, indicating that he should be quiet. He would also go downstairs to get a drink for himself and one for me. In the beginning, he would "forget" mine and keep the change for himself. It wasn't long before he would get the drinks and come back and sit in my office.

I had wondered about him often. Every now and then, I would get some word about how he was enjoying his home. He has developed quite a knack for picture taking and videography. I was really looking forward to seeing him again, but I was a little apprehensive as to what his response to seeing me might be. His huge grin, outstretched arms and that old familiar sound he'd make when he was glad to see you melted away any worry that I might have had. The only difference I noticed was that we had both aged a bit.

TOOLS YOU NEED FOR YOUR TOOL BOX:

1. Awareness that the opinions of others can be biased, and may unfairly affect the way you feel about and relate to those for whom you care

2. The ability to see and to draw upon the uniqueness of each individual person, no matter what their ability or disability

3. The realization that fear and apprehension can be healthy tools to keep you alert and aware of your situation, and that they should not be the basis for your relationship with those you serve

4. The patience to form a relationship with and to affirm and support those you serve

5. The inner strength not to become discouraged when your efforts to make a connection are not immediately acknowledged or responded to

6. The ability to be patient, consistent and honest with those you serve

7. The sensitivity to prepare those you care for when it is necessary for you to leave

8. Understanding and acceptance of people's reactions (or lack of reactions) to your leaving

POWER TOOLS:

⚓ Remember a time when someone made an unfair judgment of you. How did you feel? What, if anything, did you do or say in response? What, if anything, do you wish you had said or done? What would have been helpful?

⚓ Remember a time when you judged someone

unfairly? What motivated your judgment? Did they say or do something in response? What, if anything, did you learn from that experience? What might you do differently in a similar circumstance today?

⊛ Recall a time when someone you cared about left you or moved away. How did you feel? What, if anything, did the person do to prepare you for their leaving? If they did nothing, what would you have liked for them to have done or said? What would you like to have done or said?

Chapter Eight
THE TASK OF KNOWING WHEN TO ASK

If you are a caregiver, I want you to look at your chest. Do you see a big S there? I thought not. As much as we would like to, we cannot leap tall buildings with a single bound. We are not faster than a speeding bullet. We aren't more powerful than a locomotive. None of us possess super powers, but that doesn't stop us from trying to be all things to all people. The sad truth is that we are human, with human limitations. Because we are human, sometimes, we need help. The trick is knowing when to ask for it. Historically, I have not been good at asking for help. Hopefully, however, I'm getting better.

Time, And Eighty-one Chairs

To be truthful, it was a matter of pride to be able to do things with no assistance. My mother, wanting me to be as independent as possible, always encouraged me to learn as many skills as I could. She used to tell me, "Son, I'm not always going to be around to do things for you. I want you to be able to do as much as you can for yourself. After all, one day you'll be all grown up and living on your own, and there's no guarantee that you'll get married and have a wife to do these things for you."

Mother was right. I did need to be as independent as possible. She was a very good teacher. I can still remember her coming into my bedroom one day and asking, "Do you like to have clean sheets on your bed?" "Yes," I replied, "You know I do." "Then come with me," she said, "I'll show you how you get them." That was the day that she introduced me to the washer and dryer and taught me how to use them. I was on my way to domestic competence.

When I was in the fourth grade, my mother went to work. When she thought that I was old enough to handle it, she began to teach me how to cook. I basically learned to cook over the phone. Mother would call me on the phone after I got home from school and ask something like, "How would you like to have meat loaf, broccoli and potatoes for supper? This is what you do. If you follow my instructions and do what I tell you, when I get home, we'll have supper." Low and behold, when she got home, the meat loaf, broccoli and potatoes were ready. Surprisingly, everyone ate it and nobody died. I had made another step toward self-sufficiency.

I mention these things to make a point. When my mother was helping me to learn these different skills, she never meant to imply that I should *never* ask for help. Somewhere along the way, however, I decided that I should be able to do *everything* for myself. To illustrate just how strongly I believed this, I offer the following examples.

The first occurred while I was a summer student minister in Louisville, Kentucky. Every Sunday, I was responsible for providing worship services for several adults with developmental disabilities. Often, I would arrive for services loaded down with props and materials. On one particular Sunday, my supervisor came to observe the worship service. We arrived at the same moment. I had bags of materials in both hands, and another bag clenched between my teeth. Sizing up the situation, my supervisor said, "Here, let me help you with those things." Through clenched teeth, I replied, "No fank ou. I can ooo it mysef." Though I had difficulty accepting help from others, at that time, I didn't recognize that I had a problem in that area.

Fourteen years later, I was still pretty much a "do-it-myselfer." I had recently been transferred into the Staff Development and Training department where I currently work. Our department had been given permission to use two rooms in one of the buildings as classrooms, and we needed chairs. I told my boss that there were several chairs in the chapel balcony, which were no longer used. The flooring in the balcony contained asbestos, which resulted in the balcony being closed off. My boss asked me if I would go to the chapel and count the number of chairs in the balcony. I agreed to do so.

I climbed the stairs to the balcony, only to find that the gate, which opened into the balcony, had been padlocked. I did not have a key to fit it. I thought, briefly, about calling the locksmith on grounds to see if he could come and open the gate for me. I decided, instead, to climb over the gate. I got in with no problem. I counted the chairs. There were eighty-one. Satisfied that I had done my job, I went back to the balcony gate and prepared to climb back over.

While climbing into the balcony had presented no problem, climbing *out* was another matter. If I had lost my balance while climbing into the balcony, it would have been only three feet to the floor. Big deal. If, however, I lost my balance climbing *out* of the balcony, I would either fall through the chapel window and plunge, cut and bleeding, to my death, *or* fall down the spiral staircase, resulting, again, in my death, or a gross rearrangement of my skeletal structure. Neither option appealed to me. I was trapped. What was a self-sufficient, do-it-myselfer to do?

Suddenly, I remembered. There was a vocational workshop in the chapel basement. The staff and workshop employees were still downstairs at that time of day. What luck! Someone could call the locksmith (that *I* should have called in the first place) and set me free. All I had to do was to get their attention. I began to yell, "Help! I'm trapped in the chapel balcony!" Expectant pause. "Help! I'm trapped in the chapel balcony!" Hopeful pause. "Help! I'm trapped in the chapel balcony!" Frustrated, less than hopeful pause. Yelling was not working. What to do now?

I had a sudden flash of inspiration. Picking up a chair, I tossed it over the balcony railing. It made an impressive noise as it bounced several times on the floor below. That should have gotten someone's attention. I yelled, again. "Help! I'm trapped in the chapel balcony!" I waited. Nothing. I tossed another chair over the side. I yelled. I waited. Nothing. Just as I was about to loft another chair over the railing, I heard footsteps. The door to the back of the chapel opened, and in came Jennifer, one of the vocational staff from downstairs. She began to laugh. She looked up at me and asked, "What are you doing up *there?*" Embarrassed, I told her that I was locked in the balcony and could not get out. I asked her to please call the locksmith and ask him to come and let me out.

Laughing hysterically, Jennifer went downstairs to make the call. Within fifteen minutes, the locksmith came, unlocked the gate to the balcony, and made me a free man. Before I left the chapel, Jennifer asked me, "What would you have done if I hadn't come upstairs to find out what all the noise was about?" Smiling with embarrassment, I replied, "Time, and eighty-one chairs were on my side."

How Do You Make Holy Water?

Ever since my adventure in the balcony, asking for help when I need it hasn't seemed like such a bad idea. In fact, sometimes, when I have had the good sense to ask for assistance, I have gotten a bonus that I never expected. For example, there was a child on the hospital who was dying. His parents asked if I would baptize him before he died, and I agreed to do so. Being of a different denomination than I, the mother had one concern. "You *will* use holy water, won't you?" she asked. "Of course," I replied. She then said, "And it will be *blessed*, won't it?" "Of course," I answered, and went back to the chapel to prepare for the baptism.

Back at the chapel, it occurred to me that I didn't have the slightest idea where to get holy water, so I called a local minister of the parents' denomination. "I've been asked to do a baptism for a child who is dying, and the mother specifically asked that I use holy water," I said to my friend on the phone. "Where do I get holy water?" "You make it," came the reply. "How do I do that?" I asked in amazement. I thought that I would have to go to a store of some kind that specialized in things like holy water. "Well," said the voice on the phone, "you take a pot, fill it with water, put it on the stove and boil the hell out of it!" I was not expecting that answer. "That's it?" I asked in disbelief. "That's it," he answered. "But it has to be blessed," I said, thinking that there must be someone special whose job it was to do such mysterious things. "So, say a prayer over it," said the minister. And I did. So, you see, when you ask for help, you often get what you ask for, and, sometimes, you get a whole lot more!

THE POINTS:

➜   **We All Need Somebody To Lean On:** there is a fine line between being independent or self-sufficient, and being stubborn or pig-headed. This is true for those who give, as well as for those in need of receiving care. Caregivers sometimes need outside help to provide the best possible care for those they serve. Those in need of care and services from others often deny their need for assistance.

➜   **Know When To Hold 'UM...Know When To Fold 'Um:** Like the Kenny Rogers song, "The Gambler," persons with disabilities must be encouraged to balance independence (I can do it myself) and dependence (knowing when help is necessary). When I was a child, I would try and try and try at something, to the point of absolute frustration. I thought that asking for help was admitting that I was less of a person than everybody else. What I failed to "see," at the time, was that everybody else had times in their lives when they, too, had to ask for help. Jeff talks about a sense of **"PRIDE"** in accomplishing something on his own. Jeff, however, sometimes went to extremes in his quest for independence. While Jeff knew that he could climb *into* the chapel balcony, he failed to consider whether or not he could climb *out*. Had he paused to ask that question, he would not have ended up being stuck in the balcony. The locksmith could have unlocked the balcony gate for him. Instead, Jeff ended up trapped, with **NO WAY OUT**. He was forced to "ask" for help by throwing chairs over the edge.

➜   **Be Humble When You Bumble:** When Jeff

realized that he was stuck in the balcony, he swallowed his pride and began to call for help. Don't wait until you're stuck to ask for assistance.

➡ **Laugh When You Gaff:** When Jeff's friend, Jennifer, finally answered his call for help and came to help, she burst out laughing. Jeff did, too. Learning to take ourselves lightly when we make a mistake is a must.

➡ **Ask, And It Shall Be Given:** Jeff had no clue how or where to obtain holy water, or how or where to get it blessed. He called a minister who did, and was able to provide the grieving parents with the kind of baptismal service they desired. The more frequently you practice "asking," the more surprised you may become at how often you get what you ask for. To relinquish, to let go, may take away some of your feeling of control, but to do so will also provide you with a greater power...the ability to be vulnerable and to empathize with others.

TOOLS YOU NEED FOR YOUR TOOL BOX:

1. The ability to know your limitations
2. The ability to resist the "Superman Syndrome"
3. The courage to give up control
4. The ability to analyze a situation objectively
5. Humility
6. The courage to admit that you can't do everything by yourself
7. The wisdom to ask for help when you need it
8. The ability to laugh at yourself

POWER TOOLS:

⊛   Explore your feelings about asking for help

⊛   Think back on a time when you were in a NO
        WAY OUT situation. How did you handle it?

⊛   Think about whether it is easier for you to ask for
        help or to give help to others. What makes it easier
        to do one than the other?

Chapter Nine

WHEN CARE
LEADS TO DESPAIR

Some kinds of caregiver grief are difficult to express, and are not readily recognized by others, especially the grief that comes with the realization that, sometimes, caring isn't enough. My experience with Mrs. C. is one example of this type of caregiver grief.

Mrs. C's Story

I was talking to some of the patients on the Hemodialysis Unit at North Carolina Baptist Hospital. As a chaplain intern, I had become quite close to some of the people who came three times a week to have the toxins filtered from their blood. One was "Twinkie Man." He used to work for a local bakery, and would often bring cakes and cookies to the unit for staff and patients to enjoy. Another was Mrs. C., a grandmotherly sort, filled with warmth and charm. She was one of my favorite people.

It was the fall of the year. Evenings and early mornings had become quite cold, often below freezing. Mrs. C. and the other hemodialysis patients were easily chilled by the cold. On this particular visit, Mrs. C. told me that she had fallen that morning as she was walking to her car. Weakened by her weekly treatments, it had taken a great deal of effort for Mrs. C. to get up. She worried that the day might come when she could no longer get herself up, without assistance. Prizing her independence, she did not want to give up her home and move to an assisted living community, nor did she want to lie helpless, waiting for someone to come rescue her if she fell again. She asked me if I had any ideas.

I had recently heard of a device that a person could wear around their neck. If they needed assistance, they could push a button, alerting emergency personnel who would come to their aid. The technology was new, and no one I asked seemed to know much about the device, or how Mrs. C. might get one. Liking a challenge, I was determined to track one down for Mrs. C.

Over the next several days, I was on the phone every time I could find a spare moment. I called medical supply stores, and anyone else I could think of. Nobody had an emergency alert device. I was just about ready to give up, when I happened to find the number for a company that specialized in finding hard-to-find items for people. I dialed the number and explained what I was looking for. About an hour later, the company represent-ative called back and told me that he had located what I was looking for. He gave me the name of the supplier, and their number. I could hardly wait to give the information to Mrs. C.!

Smiling with satisfaction, I arrived at the Hemodialysis Unit in time for Mrs. C.'s treatment. She wasn't there. I asked the staff if they knew where she was, or when she would be coming. "Mrs. C. died this morning," they said quietly, still in shock. "She apparently fell while going to her car. She couldn't get up. It was very cold this morning. The EMT's said she died of exposure." I was stunned into silence, questions and feelings of guilt whirling in my mind. "Why couldn't I have worked harder to find what she needed? Why couldn't I have been faster, more efficient? Why couldn't I have found that number sooner? Why did Mrs. C. have to die alone in the cold? Why?" Later, when I was alone, I cried for Mrs. C. I cried for being too late. I cried because, sometimes, there are no answers to "why" questions.

THE POINTS:

➜ **Sometimes Our Best Fails The Test:** Sometimes, our best efforts are not enough. Though Jeff did everything he could to find the device that Mrs. C. needed, he was too late.

➜ **Stiff The "What Ifs":** When we feel that we have failed someone as a caregiver, it is normal to experience feelings of guilt, to say, "If only...,"and to ask ourselves, "What if..." questions. We often have an exaggerated feeling of responsibility for the person. We can't save everyone. Be kind to yourself.

➜ **Helplessness Brings Distress:** In the role of caregiver, we see and experience much pain. We have a tendency to want to "fix" things and make them all better. When we can't, we often feel helpless. These feelings make us very uncomfortable, but we must recognize them as part of being human. None of us like limitations, but we must learn to accept them.

TOOLS YOU NEED FOR YOUR TOOL BOX:

1. The ability to recognize and accept your limitations
2. The recognition that you can't "fix" everything
3. The ability to give yourself permission to grieve your "failures"
4. The ability to give yourself permission to grieve for those you lose

5.   The wisdom to develop a support group to get you through the difficult times

6.   The wisdom to find ways to care for yourself and recharge your caregiver batteries

POWER TOOLS:

⊕   Find a way to honor the person who died. Have a memorial service. Plant a tree, a rose bush, or a memorial garden. Get together with others who knew the person and tell stories or have a life review. Put together a photo album or a scrap book. Help the person who is dying to build a "life shrine," with items, which represent their life. Build one, which represents your life. The shrine can contain pictures, mementos, special objects, music/poetry books, candles, or anything else that represents what is important to you. It should be small enough to fit on a table top. This is an excellent group exercise.

⊕   Find ways to take care of yourself. Set aside fifteen minutes a day for "quiet time." Write a journal or a diary. Write poetry, listen to music, or develop a hobby. Take a walk in a natural setting. Spend time with your family. Love your pets. Talk to a friend. Embrace your faith.

Chapter Ten
CUSTOMIZED CARE WITH FLAIR

The very nature of the jobs that Jeff and I do, along with the fact that each of us has lifelong experience with a disability, provides us with many opportunities to get to know people with disabilities. Each situation requires its own unique solution. People are not created the same. They are not cookies cut out of dough, with a design chosen by someone else. They are individuals, shaped by their own unique life experiences. We must look at each person we encounter with open eyes and hearts, and treat them as their uniqueness requires. We need to break the cookie cutter. To do so takes unconditional love and respect. There are those we've met along the way that we will not forget.

George: George used to tell me stories about working on a farm. He helped to drive a team of horses, and would also gather the vegetables and tend the dairy cattle. He seemed to long for those days. We'd make scrapbooks about the farm, and one of his friends would make sure that he had lots of models of the animals to keep in his window. When he died, I felt it appropriate that the scrapbooks and animal models be placed in the casket with him.

Ruby: Ruby always carried a doll wherever she went. She was well into her eighties, but looked like a child, with her short stature and small features. One of her caregivers could not make it to the funeral service, but took me aside to make sure that Ruby had her doll.

Wolly: Sitting at my desk, I see the picture of Wolly that was taken several years ago. He's seated beside his girlfriend. They're holding hands and smiling. I'd known Wolly about twenty years, and was saddened to see his health/medical condition steadily deteriorating. Even in the nursing home, Wolly still remembered those things which made him happy, like his "oh yo," as he called his yo-yo, and a "harp," as he called his harmonica. When he died, I was inspired to write a poem, which I titled "The Oh Yo Man."

Once there was an "Oh Yo Man"
Sweet as he could be,
Who had a greeting for all,
But his most special was for me.

I'd bring him word from home,
As he knew the job I did.
He made my day brighter.
His smile he never hid.

And in his hand, a stuffed animal,
Or his treasured "Oh Yo."
He'd always share with others,
Never saying, "No."

Oh, how you'll be missed!
Of that have no fear.
My life's forever enriched,
Because you are so dear.

Needless to say, Wolly had both "harp" and "Oh Yo" with him in his casket.

Ernie: Everyday, I would see Ernie running back and forth on the road. He was always busy. He knew me by name, and would ask me if I had any "spare change." If I had it, he had it, but if I didn't, I'd tell him. Some of the people in the residence would get mad if you didn't have anything to give them when they asked, but not Ernie. "Next time," he would say, with a broad grin. He was a "junk food junkie," and the snack bar and store, just up the road, were his "home away from home." He was diagnosed with leukemia and was hospitalized many times. During his last hospitalization, the nurses told me that he wasn't eating, my clue that something was wrong. I went immediately to his room and asked him what he wanted to eat. "Ice cream and candy bars," was his reply. After asking the doctors if I could get these things for Ernie, I was off to the store. When I brought the ice cream and candy bars to Ernie, I never saw a happier person. He didn't eat much, but he was happy. I have far too much pocket change now, but it always serves to remind me of my dear friend, Ernie.

Ricky: We decided to take several people, who had shared a home with Ernie to his funeral. They had not been present at the hospital when he died, and we felt that this would be an opportunity for them to see him in the casket, be a part of the funeral, and get some closure. Ricky was the most vocal. He wanted to know, "Where are Ernie's shoes?" We could have explained until the cows came home, but a very kind funeral director opened the casket and showed him that Ernie had on socks. This seemed to satisfy him. He told us that Ernie would be put in a hole, and would go to Heaven. That was perfectly all right with Ricky. The funeral met with Ricky's approval, too, as it had lots of soulful singing.

Bud: It was felt that Bud understood enough to talk with Jeff and me about his wishes regarding the use of life support. He had lung cancer, from too many years of smoking, and he was facing some very difficult decisions. He had been a "rounder" in his younger years, and everybody knew that you didn't mess around with Bud. Everybody *assumed* that he was so tough, but when it came to facing his own death, *he was afraid*! The first thing that he told Jeff was that he was going to Hell. the more we talked with him, the more we were able to find out about his statement. He'd attended a local fundamentalist church for many years, and had heard that phrase used repeatedly. As Jeff and I helped Bud to see the *loving* side of God, Bud's fear of Hell and death subsided. We helped him to review his life, which included his forgiving others whom he believed had harmed him in his life, and asking for the forgiveness of others that he believed he had harmed. He decided against artificial life support, and his death was a peaceful one.

Eva: A fellow employee, Mike, told Jeff and me the story of the lengthy friendship between two ladies with developmental disabilities, living in the community. One of the ladies had recently died, and the other approached Mike at a time when he was swamped with work needing to be finished *yesterday*. He could have told her to come back later, because he was so busy. He chose, instead, to invite Eva into his office, and waited patiently while, with many tears shed, she painstakingly dug through nearly everything in her huge pocket book until, finally, she proudly displayed the picture of her and her friend, taken several years ago. Once the picture was found, Eva seemed happier. She got up and went on her way. What would have happened if Mike had not bothered to listen? Fortunately, we will never know.

THE POINTS:

➜ **Free To Be Me:** Persons with developmental disabilities are individuals. Each person brings their own personality and coping skills to situations of grief, bereavement and loss. George grieved the loss of his life on the farm. Bud was afraid that he was going to Hell. Eva just wanted someone to listen to her tell the story of her friend who had died. Ricky simply wanted to know where Ernie's shoes were. Just as each individual was different, so were his or her needs. Sounds a lot like you and me, doesn't it?

➜ **Tailor Made Care/Customized Comfort:** there is no computer generated **PLAN** to be used for everyone who has suffered grief, bereavement or loss. Each situation calls for creativity, flexibility, patience, understanding that responses will vary, and a clear picture of **WHO** you are providing care for. Scrapbooks of farm life and model animals made George's last days more bearable. Wolly had his "oh yo" and harp. Caring for Ernie was as simple as knowing his favorite types of ice cream and candy bars, and making sure he had them. He may have taken only a few bites of each, but his smile and "Thank you, Carolyn" let me know that the pain he suffered from leukemia was somewhat lessened. Ricky would not have been satisfied unless he had seen Ernie's feet. The funeral director agreed to open the bottom portion of the casket so that Ricky could see. Bud was fearful and anxious, thinking that he was going to Hell when he died, because of the bad things he had done to others. Jeff and I helped him to see the loving side of God, and assisted him with a "Life Review," by gathering together those persons Bud felt he had hurt, as well as those who had hurt him. He was able to experience the healing power of giving and receiving forgiveness. Bud was then able to relinquish his "hold" on life and die peacefully. Mike, a fellow employee, listened patiently (though his work needed to be done *yesterday*) and gave Eva permission to talk about the death of her best friend.

➜   **Death With Dignity:** When you think about death with dignity, pain management is one of the first things you might think of. This is a very important piece of the puzzle. Without pain management, other comfort measures will be compromised. End of Life decisions, such as whether to use CPR, antibiotics, or blood transfusions, which can result in prolonging the inevitable, affect the life or death of the individual and the lives of the next of kin and the caregivers. These decisions are very difficult, and are approached very differently, depending on a person's religious beliefs, as well as moral and ethical beliefs. Whenever there are next of kin, the End of Life decisions will be made by the physician and them. their decisions may conflict with what you, the caregiver, believe. The law may tell you one thing, but your heart and emotions will often tell you just the opposite.

➜   **Treasure In Earthen Vessels:** Each of these "snapshots" has provided you with a glimpse of several persons with disabilities that Jeff and I have had the pleasure to serve and to love. There are other stories, too numerous to mention. Do not take away from individuals in death, that which was precious to them in life.

George's scrapbooks and models, Wolly's "oh yo" and harp, and Ruby's doll were buried with them. After one of our residents died in the hospital, we discovered that his Barney, that he was never without, had been left behind. A quick call was made to the funeral home to tell them that we were on our way with Barney. He had a prominent place among the flowers at the graveside, and was placed in the casket after the service.

TOOLS YOU NEED FOR YOUR TOOL BOX:

1. The ability to recognize that there are different responses to grief, bereavement and loss, due to individual personalities, feelings, religious beliefs

2. The ability to be creative, flexible, patient and understanding, rather than relying on a "canned plan"

3. Knowledge of the person you are serving, including their likes and dislikes, and familiarity with how they react in stressful situations

4. Willingness to advocate for pain management when appropriate

5. The ability to accept the fact that you may not have the final say concerning End of Life decisions

6. Awareness that your religious, ethical or moral beliefs may conflict with the beliefs of others

7. Respect for the religious, ethical or moral beliefs of others

8. Awareness of the difficulty of making End of Life decisions

9.   Respect for the End of Life decisions made, even when you may not agree with the decision made
10.   Empathy for those making End of Life decisions
11.   Clear awareness of your role of caregiver, and awareness of who you are caring for
12.   Willingness to take part in celebrating the person's life, whether it is by telling a story, or making sure that their "something special" is buried with them
13.   All the above points regarding end of life are made with the assumption that there is clear understanding of the difference between "disease" and "disability". One's life should not be ended just because one has a disability. Disability is NOT a lifelong disease. Disability is simply another way of being. Confusing "disability" with "disease" will give parents and careproviders an excuse to commit murder. This is not an extreme statement ... it has been done.

POWER TOOLS:

14.   If you do not have one, draw up an advanced directive/living will

15.   Plan your funeral/memorial service

16.   Write your obituary

17.   Remember some "snapshots" of persons you have served who have died. How did you make them comfortable? Did they have death with dignity? (If not, how could that have been accomplished? How might you help to ensure that those you serve experience death with dignity in the future?) Were

there any conflicts surrounding End of Life issues? How were they resolved? If there were unresolved conflicts, how might similar conflicts be resolved in the future? What did you learn from the conflict situation(s)?

18.   Write down what you want on your tombstone (and we're not talking about pizza).

Jeff and I hope that you have enjoyed sharing some of our stories and experiences, and that you have found something of value within these pages to take away for yourself. We would like to close this chapter and this book with one last quote. For us, it seems to capture the essence of what it means to be a caregiver.

The caregiver...cares
By not trying to change or cure.
In allowing for that which seems
To be intolerable,
And in accepting that which looks like
It is unacceptable,
The caregiver...
Is a true giver of care.

"The Tau of Dying"
Douglas C. Smith

Carolyn Bowling is a graduate of Virginia Commonwealth University, in Richmond, Virginia, with a Masters of Science in Rehabilitation Counseling. She has been a Social Worker since 1974, serving individuals with developmental disabilities in Lynchburg, Virginia. She currently works for the Department of Mental Health/Mental Retardation and Substance Abuse Services, in an Acute Care and a Nursing Facility Care Unit, serving patients, their families and hospital staff. Her interest in grief, bereavement and loss issues among people with disabilities comes from both personal and professional experience. She conducts seminars on grief, bereavement and loss with her friend and colleague, Jeff Wilder. Carolyn is an avid cat lover, earning her the nickname, "Cat Woman". She also sings in a band called "Old Stuff". Carolyn lives with her mother and her cat, Trouble.

Jeff Wilder is a graduate of East Carolina University, in Greenville, North Carolina, with a BA in Psychology. He is also a graduate of The Southern Baptist Theological Seminary, in Louisville, Kentucky, with a M.Div. Jeff has served as a Chaplain for the Department of Mental Health/Mental Retardation and Substance Abuse Services in Lynchburg, Virginia, working with people with developmental disabilities, their families, and staff. Since 1992, he has also worked as a Staff Development and Training Instructor. Like Carolyn, his interest in grief, bereavement and loss issues among people with disabilities comes from personal and professional experience. Jeff lives with his wife, Debbie, and his two sons, Justin and Ryan. He enjoys singing, reading, and working with people.

ABOUT THE ANGEL ON THE COVER

A lovely lady named Diane is our cover artist. Diane is a very talented artist who just happens to be deaf have a developmental disability. She has lived in a residential facility in Virginia for the past 45 years. In 1997, staff working with Diane introduced her to painting. When watching her paint, the enjoyment she gets from creating works of art is evident. The look of purposeful intensity in her eyes is unmistakable. As you can see by the cover, Diane has a wonderful sense of color. Originally, the subject of her painting was a doll. Diane decided that the doll would look better as an angel. We agree. Carolyn and I would like to express our appreciation to Diane for allowing us to grace the cover of our book with her lovely angel.